Chad playing his guitar on the porch

REMEMBERING TO DANCE

REMEMBERING TO DANCE

Barbara H Mullen Reed, EdD

Remembering to Dance

Copyright © 2017 by Barbara H Mullen Reed

All rights reserved.

No part of this book may be reproduced in any form or by any electronic or mechanical means including information storage and retrieval systems, without permission in writing from the author. The only exception is by a reviewer, who may quote short excerpts in a review.
Book design by Barbara H Mullen Reed

Front Cover Image:
Back Cover Image:

Back Page Author Photograph: Barbara H Mullen Reed

This is a Fictional Memoir
Written by Barbara H Mullen Reed
Visit my website at www.barbarareedauthor.com

Printed in the United States of America
First Printing: September 2017
Published by: Sojourn Publishing, LLC

ISBN: 978-1-62747-150-3
ebook ISBN: 978-1-62747-152-7

Dedicated, with deep appreciation to Chad, my Dad, to Chad, my son, and to Chad Mayer.

These three remarkable people named Chad have joined me on my life path, each at just the right time, from my birth to the present moment.

They have shared with me their gifts from Divine Source of happiness, courage, wisdom, and love. Namaste.

Contents

Introduction xi

Part I
Chapter 1: Los Niños de la Calle 12/1989 to 01/1991 3
Chapter 2: Celebration of a New Year, 1992 13
Chapter 3: January, 1992 The Journey Home 17
Chapter 4: January, 1992 Meeting 21

Part II
Chapter 1: October, 1995 New Life 33
Chapter 2: October, 1995 Love in Action 39
Chapter 3: November, 1995 Advent Journey 43
Chapter 4: December, 1995 The Market 47
Chapter 5: December, 1995 Posada 53
Chapter 6: December 1995 Hiding in Plain Sight 59
Chapter 7: Christmas, 1995 63
Chapter 8: December, 1995 Ordinary Miracles 73
Chapter 9: December, 1995 Reunion 77
Chapter 10: December 28, 1995 Holy Innocents 83
Chapter 11: December, 1995 A Sanctuary
  Movement Priest 87
Chapter 12: December, 1995-January,
  1996 Sanctuary 91
Chapter 13: January, 1996 Lessons 97
Chapter 14: January, 1996 Hope 99
Chapter 15: January, 1996 Feast of the Three Kings 105
Afterword 111
Notes 113

Introduction
Vision and Direction
November 1995

I am sitting at the mouth of a spacious cave, holding a bowl filled with clear, fresh water from the stream below. It is a smooth, brown bowl made from banana leaves and corn husks that have been soaked in water from the river and molded by hand into graceful curves, then patiently dried in the sun. There is a braided rim of reeds around the edge of the bowl that has Mayan symbols woven through it. I love the texture and graceful artistry of this bowl. I treasure it because it was crafted by hand by friends in the village, and given to me as a gift, many months ago.

It has been almost four years since I arrived at the place I now call home. What started as a two-week trip, planned with a colleague to explore Guatemala, underwent a dramatic shift that has changed the course of my life. It began with a casual conversation at a church-related gathering in Florida. The woman who was going to Guatemala to gather data for an article on the lives of the children of the street (Los Niños de la Calle) in Guatemala City wanted me to go with her. She spoke fluent Spanish. I managed to speak and understand at probably an intermediate college Spanish level, and would truly welcome her assistance.

It was a sad time for me in my personal life. My youngest son, Chad, a gentle giant with a flair for leadership and good humor, had died at age twenty-six in a tragic accident. I could see him now in my mind's eye, well over six feet tall, with shaggy blonde hair, clear blue eyes, and a big smile. My soulmate, best friend, and partner, Annie, was, by contrast, exactly five feet in height, with her blonde/gray hair in a ponytail and a sparkle in her eyes. She was ready with deeply insightful and delightfully humorous commentary in every situation. She didn't let her height hold her back. I had seen her, on occasion, climb up to address a group from a table top if they seemed to be "looking down" on her. Annie presented a definite contrast to Chad in appearance, but she was just as outgoing, with great enthusiasm for life. She was a lawyer who did pro bono work for those who couldn't afford to pay. Chad was a teacher and a volunteer community builder. Annie had made the transition to the world just beyond ours as a result of a fast-acting cancer, suddenly diagnosed, that swept her away within five weeks of its onset.

As we discussed the Guatemala trip, I was immediately caught up in the possibility of a change of scene, unexpected as it was, and agreed on the spot to purchase an airline ticket to Guatemala City and to make sure my passport was in order. My job as a part-time substitute teacher/volunteer at the local parish church would be there when I returned.

I believe that there is no such thing as death as a finality or as an ending. I feel with certainty the presence of my loved ones who have transitioned to the "Land of the Spirits," also known as "Heaven." Even so, I was struggling with their passing and deeply mourning their absence in human form. The sudden loss of their physical presence was devastating to me. Tears came uninvited at unexpected moments. At the same time, I was constantly given the gift of indisputable evidence that they were close by and loving me still. Chad seemed to be playing his guitar and singing with gusto. I could picture him telling jokes and getting everyone around him singing too. The message was that he was fine, even though he didn't address me directly. Annie surrounded me with love and a beautiful image of light. In a dream, she showed me how she would appear if she reclaimed her human body. It was an image of pain and struggle to survive. Then she showed me the difference in the transition to her present form as Spirit, and how she literally radiated light and perfect health. She smiled and held me in her radiance and let me know that she was going to stay close to me.

These gifts of remembrance were creating healing every day, but the psychic pain of the overwhelming loneliness never moved far from my consciousness. The adventure in Guatemala, well planned and simple in scope, would be ideal. It would be a diversion in which I hoped to be of service. We would even visit at least one place where Chad had travelled when he had been chipping away at rock and helping to prepare a site for a school in the mountains in the eastern part of the country, several hours by bus from the City. All of the pieces were falling into place.

Such is the illusion of order and certainty in our mortal lives. As it happened, my adventure was to be far different from the one I had imagined. The woman who had invited me to accompany her telephoned with her apologies the DAY before we were to leave. Her daughter needed her for an emergency, and she had to cancel. My passport was ready; my airline ticket was not refundable.

It took an hour of quiet meditation on my part to obtain the clear answer that I was to go ahead with the plan to travel to Guatemala. Yes, I decided to go alone to an unknown destination. There was no guidance at that time as to where I was to travel once I arrived at the airport. I was not interested in a tourist experience or a tour. I looked at a map; asked a few questions of friends and family who had visited the country before me. I decided to add a few necessary things to my backpack, fly to Guatemala City, and keep the appointments related to the visits at Casa Alianza, where I would spend time on the streets with volunteers helping children. I would not schedule or limit my time for this activity. I would volunteer along with the others for as long as I could be of assistance. From there, I would travel by bus for about eight hours to the Rio Dulce. Then, after a short motorboat ride down the scenic river, I would hike to the mountains above it. From that point, I would follow no set route or plan. I was used to hiking. I was physically fit and able bodied. I would rely on my proven DGS (Divine Guidance System) to take me wherever I was destined to go.

Now, four years later, I sit at the entrance to this beautiful and mysterious cave. This is a place of quiet majesty. It is an ideal place for just resting and dreaming and praying. There are so many things that are right and just in the world, and I decide to mentally list and give thanks for each of them.

For the past week, I have been walking the five miles here each morning from the mountain village, where I am a guest. No, I am more than a guest, I am part of the close-knit community that calls the village home. I feel such deep friendship for each person there, like a beloved sister, me to them and they to me.

This is a week of soul searching for me. It is a season of contemplation and prayer as I prepare for something that I can only imagine is about to happen. I feel a sort of intuition that challenges are coming and that I am meant to prepare for them. I have asked for a vision, a message, to give me an indication if there is something that I am destined to do. Often, when I sit quietly in prayer and meditation – just surrendering to the guidance of Divine Source that is my beacon through the Universe – images and words gather in my thoughts. I don't plan or design them; they just drop in like snow, softly and gently falling, or small stars landing and glowing brightly with messages of hope and encouragement. This experiencing and knowing have been part of who I am from my earliest recollections as a small child.

There is a beautiful little stream flowing nearby. It tumbles over rocks and then forms a deep, clear pool before dashing off again over more rocks on its way down the mountain. I strip off my clothes and bathe in it daily, and then wash my clothes and spread them out to dry on the rocks that line the bank. I sit on a flat-topped rock in the sun near my drying clothes, and I feel the gentle breeze stroking my skin and ruffling my hair. The pleasant warmth of the day permeates my body and seems to bring the sunlight inside of me. There it acts as a sort of radiant developer that processes my thoughts and feelings, and brings an inner glow of peace and gratitude for all that is.

This is surely a place for meditation and inspiration. When the clothes are almost dry (the humidity keeps them from drying completely, even in the sun), I put them back on and move toward the entrance to the large cave, carved out of the rock face of the mountain, about a half-mile uphill from the stream. There is a smooth glacial formation that forms the floor of the cave and extends outward as a sort of shelf on which one can sit and observe the surrounding area. It is a natural resting place, as well as a vantage point for seeing beyond one's immediate surroundings. I look out over the vastness of the forest. I drink from the bowl that I am holding, and then I set it aside.

It is dusk, so I will be staying here tonight, since it isn't safe to travel through the forest in the dark. I am content to spend the night here in this magical cave, where many have lived in years past.

It is time to prepare for the night. I have stored a bedroll in the cave. I take out a blanket and spread it on the flat rock outside. I make a quick survey and find that I have enough firewood and kindling to build a fire.

Taking matches from my stash in the bedroll, I gather kindling together, place it under and around the logs, and start the fire outside the cave in the usual place on the ledge. As I sit on the colorful blanket, woven with intricate Mayan symbols by Colel, my sister in Spirit from the village, I feel the air grow much cooler. I stand briefly, pull on my sweater and raise my arms in a joyful salute to the moon and the stars that are appearing in the night sky. I sit back down and stay especially quiet, listening to the crackling of the fire and inhaling the earthy smell as the logs begin to glow. As I sit, I became aware of a deep silence drawing me in. I surrender completely any temptation to "think" or even to imagine.

The summer days are warm and humid in the mountains and forests above the Rio Dulce, and the nights are extremely cool. A fire is necessary for warmth, and it also adds a dimension of connection with the four elements honored by the ancestors of the Mayan people. There is the earth, the air, water, and fire. It has always been the Mayan belief that these are the sacred elements that connect all living beings to each other and to the universe. These are the essentials for life. As I drift through this deep experience of being one with the people and with the earth and being guided by the Universe, I feel a peacefulness and a joy beyond description.

As I sit in the power of this stillness, I sense a gentle movement of the air and know that the Spirit of my dearest friend, Annie, has joined me. I also feel encircled by the comforting presence of my Spirit Guides encircling me. They connect me to the Universe, to everything that is known to us, and to that which is still beyond our human understanding.

It has been our belief that the Spirit of each living thing lives on eternally, and that some of these wise Spirits who now dwell in the astral plane many call Heaven are sent out to act as spiritual helpers to those still inhabiting the planet in the form we recognize as "living beings." These helpers we refer to as refer to as our Spirit guides. Departed loved ones are also nearby. There is my little daughter, April whose soul passed to this other world at birth my dear Grandmother, who nurtured a spirit of creativity within me, and my dear son, Chad, and of course, Annie every one of whom blessed me with the gift of unconditional love. I consider each of them to be closely connected to me always. In addition, there are our loved ones who stay near us with whom we can lovingly connect, and they with us.

I feel Annie's presence, as I often do. She sits close to me, and I sense her smile. I imagine that we join arms and hands. We sit together, silently watching the spirits of many people who have passed to the next world go by – the Guatemalan people who were driven by wars of conquest out of the rich valleys and up into the mountains far from their homes, and died on the way; the babies and toddlers stolen from their parents to be sold as orphans for adoption by families in the United States, and did not survive; the addicted children paid in toxic glue to beg on the streets for coins for their masters; the young boys and girls who do not often survive their childhood. We cry for them, and we mourn with them. The Spirits have joined us in this reflection on the heartbreaking history of this place of beauty and of courage. Words are felt rather than spoken.

As our prayer continues, I sense Annie is saying to me, "We haven't done what is most essential... we haven't danced to celebrate their lives and to show them that they are loved. How can their spirits stay fully alive without being surrounded by joy?"

We rise as one and dance around the fire, at first just swaying slowly in rhythm with the movement of the Spirits passing by, and then they begin to dance with us. I seem to hear the steady beat of a ceremonial drum, and the clear tone of a flute. We move together and become part of a shifting of bodies and images of shapes and shadows. This is not a dance of despair, but a dance that is filled with joyful leaping and graceful movement. We feel connected to every dimension and to Divine Source. It is a beautiful expression of the meaning of the fullness of life and an experience with a whole range of possibilities, yet with no firm conclusions.

Whether we who are earth residents are awake or asleep, the Spirits of those who are walking in the next world come in meditation and present vital messages. There is often an urgency to these messages, encouraging the recipients to do everything we can to bring joy and love to each of the inhabitants of the earth. It's a gentle prodding, urging us to do our part to overcome and replace the all-too-frequent ethic of domination in our planetary home with the ethic of love.

At the cave, I am encouraged to enter into the joy of possibilities, and to dance in celebration and anticipation. I am asked to take the Spirit of the fire with me into my heart and soul, and to be light to every other that I meet.

The music and the dancers fade, but the feelings of inner joy and connectedness and the promise of unlimited possibility remain. It is once again very quiet, except for the sounds of the movement of the tree branches and the conversations of the birds and animals of the night. I bring my blankets and sleeping mat to the mouth of the cave and bank the fire for the night. As I drift off to sleep, wrapped in the warm blankets, I feel the gentle presence of my Spirit guides, and this brings me comfort and peace. Why and how this happens, I cannot say for sure. I just know that they are never "lost" or "missing," and that every day they encourage me to envision dancing in gratitude for and with the earth – and for every living being, past and present.

When daylight returns, I still feel at peace. After performing my daily bathing and laundry rituals in the stream and preparing the cave for my departure, I take my bedroll and backpack and start out on the walk back to the village. I think of the day I originally arrived there, and of the divine guidance that sent me in that direction.

I know now that there is no other message I need to hear. I was sent to that village, and I am there for a reason. Any further purpose will become clear in perfect timing. I accept this with my heart and soul, and I release any doubts as to whether I can successfully meet whatever challenges arise. I walk back home, thinking of those early days of travelling to the village before I even knew it existed.

I invite you, the reader, to join me now in the retelling of the tale of that journey and of the events that have followed.

PART I

Chapter 1
Los Niños de la Calle
December 1989 to January 1991

It was a warm, sunny day on which I began what was to be the first leg of my journey. I, a tall, pale-skinned native of the United States with a Scandinavian heritage, followed my heart with great excitement, and some trepidation, and set out to travel around the country of Guatemala.

My flight was direct from Miami on Aviateca Airlines, which is based in Guatemala City. The first sight of the city from the air offered a clear view of the Incienso Bridge, the highest road bridge in Guatemala, which is considered to be somewhat of an engineering wonder. In stark contrast, there was also an aerial view of the sprawling disaster that is the largest landfill in Central America. I had read that amid garbage and the acrid fumes of burning piles of trash, much of it contaminated by harsh chemicals, several thousand men, women, and children reside in makeshift structures – such as pieces of cardboard boxes – that they call home. There is no running water, and of course there are no sanitary facilities. Tragically, residents are at the mercy of the street gangs, and to be marginalized to the point of being forced to live there is to barely survive. This view of the city is shattering in its stark reality.

Within minutes, we landed, and I was actually in Guatemala. La Aurora International Airport was a vast place of organized chaos. It was December, the beginning of the warm, relatively dry season that is considered to be prime time for a vacation in Guatemala. The passage through immigration and customs was smooth. I had no checked luggage, just my backpack, so I was quite quickly able to join the surging crowd making inquiries at the ground transportation center. I asked directions and quickly located the bus that would take me closest to the budget hotel where I would be staying. I felt a mixture of anticipation in being part of the colorful, festive scene, and of lingering sadness arising from the view of El Basurero Dump Site. I had seen from the plane. I had "passed over" this atrocity in a comfortable seat in an airplane. I felt the helplessness of being part of the cause of the inequalities in the world, and I felt at the same time a firm and loving bond to everyone living in that hell on earth. I was a sister to every one of them, from the youngest baby to the street gang members. But I was their sister in exile.

From the airport, I took the bus to the corner nearest to the Spring Hotel. The small hotel would serve as my "city home" for whatever period of time I was in the vast expanse of Guatemala's capital. In spite of my sometimes-faulty inner compass, I made it from the bus stop to the hotel with no detours. The Spring can be described as a combination of a budget hotel and a youth hostel. Shared baths with hot and cold running water, clean sheets, and insect-free mattresses are definite pluses. There is a lovely, inexpensive coffee shop attached, with a pleasant patio area.

I sat in the café and wrote in my journal, and drank a cup of the delicious coffee. Then upstairs in my room, I checked over my camera, a Canon EOS 10, and made sure I had enough rolls of film in the case. I charged the spare battery, and packed everything in preparation for the next morning. Sleep came quickly, and before I knew it, the alarm was telling me it was 5 AM. Friends have often asked how I can drink coffee and then immediately go to sleep in an unfamiliar place. I attribute it to characteristics I must have mimicked from ancient travelling companions such as wolves. One of the animals stays on watch and the others just rejuvenate for the next leg of the journey by circling the sleeping area to check for hazards, and then flopping down and sleeping soundly until it is time to move on.

The shower was a great way to wake up. I had washed my clothes in the hot water the night before. They were almost dry, so dressing was just a bit sticky. I pulled on the backpack and anchored the camera case so that it could not be slipped off my shoulder by a passerby. The next stop was in the courtyard, where I sat on a bench and meditated for about thirty minutes and came to a peaceful place from which I could venture out into the day that lay ahead. I felt strongly the energy of my Spirit Guides, and their support for whatever came next.

After a fast coffee and a bun, I went down the street to Casa Alianza. Casa Alianza (known as Covenant House in the United States) was undergoing a major change, in fact a crisis, in its governance. The founder and international director had resigned under a cloud of accusations that he had misappropriated funds, and that he and some of the employees in various branches of the organization around the world had engaged in illicit sexual activities with some of the young boys that they claimed to be sheltering from life on the streets.

The staff of the facility in Guatemala had been thoroughly investigated and rearranged as necessary. It had been a huge blow to Covenant House, as it had led a charmed life for many years, had taken in many millions of dollars, and had allegedly rehabilitated and helped countless numbers of children living on the streets of many cities. That reputation was now almost completely eradicated, and donations were dropping fast.

Outside the high iron gate in front of the shelter, I was surrounded by small children with dirt-streaked hands and faces, ragged and filthy clothing, and constant demands for coins. My blond hair, blue eyes, and fair skin served to make me a standout amid the sea of brown faces. I, smiled and gently extricated myself from their midst. I wanted to sit down and talk with them, but this didn't seem realistic at the moment. An employee immediately answered my request to enter the facility. He shooed the children aside, admitted me to the front yard, and closed and locked the gate behind me. I looked around and saw a well-maintained building with an attractive flower garden and a stone path leading to the front door.

The door opened, and we entered a wide hallway that had the look of a residence rather than an institution. Everything was orderly and there was an odor of Pine-Sol and prevailing cleanliness. The employee summoned the acting director, who introduced himself as Jose Torres, and we spent about thirty minutes talking in his office. Jose was of average height with brown eyes; straight, black, shoulder-length hair; and a genuine, warm smile. He explained the programs to me, and we discussed some of the challenges posed by the scandals that had damaged the reputation of the organization and resulted in changes in leadership. The scandals had also brought a lack of confidence among donors that Casa Alianza could survive. We agreed that, of course, the children would be the ones who would suffer if the facility closed.

The streets in the city are dangerous. Another child had been killed by a street gang that morning. He had been one who was not admitted to the shelter, as he refused to follow the one rule for entry. He would have had to agree to receiving assistance in giving up the glue to which he was addicted. The gates of the shelter would open to admit any child who would agree to treatment – which started with agreeing to be weaned from drugs under medical supervision.

Jose Torres left the room for a moment and returned with two women. Leticia, a slender woman of about five feet five inches in height, looked up at me with earnest black eyes framed by long lashes. She smiled, and her face lit up with an openness and kindness that instantly drew me to want to hear more of her life story. Leticia told me that she had grown up in a conservative Roman Catholic family in Guatemala City, had graduated from the local University, and was dedicated to the ministry with the children on the streets of Guatemala. The other young woman was about my height, five feet nine inches. She was a slender blonde with fair skin and a contagious smile. Her blue eyes sparkled with enthusiasm as she described her role on the team of young professionals working with the children. She was a graduate student from the Netherlands, taking courses in international relations at Universidad Francisco Marroquín on a fellowship.

Her name was Betje. They were about to go out on their daily route around the city, to be with the children living on the streets. The materials they carried with them were small story books, a pad and pencils, and first-aid supplies. I was welcome to go with them and to take photos or record a video. I agreed at once. Before we left, the women showed me around the facility, which looked comfortable and well run. The kitchen was well equipped and the dining room looked like a friendly place. Children were being taught in three cheerful classrooms. They looked interested and even happy. The bedrooms each held two sets of bunk beds and there were well-maintained showers and toilets. Upon graduation, graduates of this elementary-level program would move to a facility for older children. There was also a school near Antigua, they explained, where students at the high school level could learn farming.

Once we were outside, children recognized the women and immediately crowded around, with everyone talking at once. We walked to a park, and when the children and adults were seated on the grass or around the fountain, Betje went from person to person, applying first aid where needed, while Leticia began to read a story in Spanish to a delighted group of the children. Their ages ranged from about five to twelve years of age. I took photos and started a video. There were no parents of whom to ask permission, so I took a chance that I would somehow be allowed to share the crucial message back home in the United States, even if only within small groups.

The children, without exception, carried rags soaked in the toxic glue, which they inhaled from necessity. Once begun, their habit had to be maintained. Stopping suddenly without adequate detox and medical assistance could result in sudden and violent death. The maintenance was provided each night in one of the many dark alleyways of the city. The price that had to be paid was to turn over to the drug supplier all of the money that the child had collected by begging on the street that day. The reward was enough glue for the next day, and admission to a tiny, filthy room filled with small children and fetid air, where for a few hours, the young addict could sleep on the floor with the others, away from the dangers of the streets.

The most lucrative form of "sponsored" begging was the child who was physically disabled either at birth, or through torture upon capture, when limbs might be amputated. The child would be rolled out daily to lie on a flat board with small wheels. He or she would usually be placed along a street of shops, with a container positioned on the wheeled board beside the child for donations from sympathetic passersby. The proceeds would be collected at the end of each day by the child's owner, and he or she would receive their glue allotment and some water and bread.

Betje and Leticia are part of a group of compassionate and caring volunteers who spend some of each day with the children. They can't be with each group for long, as the children could be punished if they fell short of their expected collections for that day. The women see that their presence makes a difference. Leticia told me that she was raised in a strict Catholic household, and that she went through every one of the religious-training classes at her parish church. Her family lives in one of the wealthier areas, and she was protected from seeing the life on the streets. As she studied, she began to hear the gospel message and to realize that there were some clear instructions as to compassion and justice.

As Leticia put it, "I saw that in order to say convincingly, 'God is love,' you couldn't just speak the words. You had to apply them to your life, and to live them. You had to actually be the unconditional love that comes from God."

After Leticia graduated from college, she decided to work part time for at least a year, and to put her religious studies into practice, by becoming acquainted with the children living on the streets and those living at the dump that I had observed from the plane. The year that she set aside has now extended for four additional years. She cannot stop, she said, as the need is so great. She has just been offered a full-time position at Casa Alianza, training those who will go out on the streets. She loves the children as if they were part of her family. Her mother and father are perplexed at her choice, but they love and respect her for what she has chosen to do. People ask if she is afraid to be exposed to the violence of the streets. She answers that dangers can come to anyone, anywhere. What better place to face the possible end of your life than bandaging a wound, or holding a child in your arms!

Our last stop each day was the street that is called "El Hoyo" (the Hole). It is located at the back of the area where most of the produce trucks come in to set up and sell at the central market within the city. On this street are many houses of prostitution and buildings with dingy, dirty rooms whose owners charge a fee per night to the drug dealers. Glue or thinner is provided to the children, and a small space on the floor in which to sleep. Fifteen to twenty children are crowded into each tiny room. These are the same children who roam the streets begging for coins by day. They spend each day dirty, lethargic, and perpetually high.

Leticia, Betje and others go out each day with their first-aid kit and books and games. The children love them, and crowd around as soon as they see them. One of the boys we met today had a badly infected puncture wound on his foot. Another had an infected machete wound on his head. Each was treated gently with water, antiseptic, and a bandage. That was the extent of the medical assistance that could be offered on the street. Both boys were polite and grateful, but each refused to go for further treatment. Leticia said that the two of them sometimes treat seventy children a day.

The frustration of the dead-end results, is shared by the Department of Social Services. Their solution is to have periodic sweeps of the city, in which they pick up as many children as their trucks will hold and transport them to a large State orphanage, or to Casa Alianza. This stopgap measure lasts only for a day or two. Casa Alianza cannot accommodate children who are actively practicing their addiction, and the children who are addicted aren't willing to submit to treatment. They are quickly released from the orphanage, and from Casa Alianza, back onto the street – and the problem is not solved, but perpetuated.

The Child Services Department criticizes Casa Alianza for going out to the children on the streets and treating their wounds, etc. even though they are still drug involved. The department would prefer that the volunteers lecture the children on "giving up glue and getting a job." As Jose Torres said, "The problem is not the children on the street. It is the socioeconomic system that puts and keeps so many in poverty so that so few can prosper."

Both Leticia and Betje told me that they often feel so powerless in the face of the realities of life on the streets. There seems to be no solution, no way out of the ongoing tragedy. It feels like putting a small Band-Aid on a life-threatening wound.

We spent several hours with various groups of children. They let me help with the first aid and the storytelling and the art work. It was fun to enter into the spirit of the moment, and just celebrate being with the children without needing to agonize over possible solutions. It was a beautiful day. Emotionally, each day was utterly exhausting. It is something that never becomes routine.

As we walked back to the shelter, Betje and Leticia asked if I could come again tomorrow. I said I would, of course. Jose Torres was delighted. He said that he hoped I would come every day, and maybe teach some classes at the shelter too. I smiled at that, but gave no promises. The days would unfold one at a time.

Betje and Leticia had told me that there was a dark secret in the city that was connected with –and yet separate from – the tragedy of the addicted children who were owned by drug dealers. That was the market for the sale of babies and young children, who were often kidnapped by the teenaged gangs of street dwellers. I had worked behind the scenes in the Sanctuary Movement in Florida, and I knew some of this. As we walked through the La Hoya area, they showed me how it often happened. The children of villagers who came to sell at the City market would play in back of the market stalls, while the parents were busy making sales for their subsistence lifestyle. The street children emerging from the sleeping rooms that bordered that street would join the children at play – and soon there would be the danger of drugs for those visiting, and the temptation for one of the older gang members to grab one of the market children and disappear with them. There was a ready market for the sale of both healthy babies and healthy older children. They would be classified as "orphans" and would be sold to wealthy families in the United States who were childless – and who had no idea that the child they paid a large sum to adopt, through an agency in Guatemala, actually had living parents.

After two weeks, I cancelled my return airline ticket. For the next year, I went out each day with one of the volunteer teams. I mailed letters and copies of the developed photos to the people in the church group in Florida who wanted to write updates on the shelter programs. One of them sent money to the hotel each month to pay my bill (about $300 per month). I was living in Guatemala, doing work that I loved, and now I was able to speak fluent Spanish. I thought that skill would be a great help when I went to the River and climbed into the mountains to visit the villages. I was exceptionally happy to be where I was. It was better to be on the scene of a disaster than to be thinking about it from afar. The timing was right. Our teams could freely roam the streets and parks with the children. We could not rearrange the government, but we could love the children struggling to survive in what seemed to be an impossible situation, and be there with them and they with us for part of each day.

Chapter 2
Celebration of a New Year, 1992

Leticia and Betje believed in taking breaks from the grim life on the street, in order to maintain the positive energy needed to survive the constant assault on the senses of the tragedy of the children's existence. As the time for me to leave the city for the countryside arrived, they insisted that I join them in celebrating New Year's Eve. We would be traveling to the ancient tourist city of Antigua, where they would meet up with friends from the university. I was prepared to set off on the next phase of my journey, but the Antigua trip with them sounded too good to miss.

We took a bus to Antigua. Most of the twenty-eight miles were an ascent into the mountains, reaching an elevation of 5,200 feet. The scenery was breathtaking, and I could see why visitors to Guatemala like the tourist areas. The view from the bus windows presented a world that was in stark contrast to the conditions in the City. The mountains were more beautiful than I could have imagined. Among the majestic peaks were several usually inactive volcanoes, though this former capital of the country has been destroyed more than once by earthquakes and volcanic eruptions. The volcanoes were picturesque, though definitely to be respected for their potential. Small farms dotted the valleys. It was a relaxing ride, and a welcome change of pace.

When we arrived at our destination, it was amazing to me that my traveling companions could find their friends in the mass of humanity that had poured onto the cobblestone streets of the city. People of all ages filled the streets – laughing, calling out to each other, and celebrating the end of one year and the beginning of the next. There were food vendors and musicians on every corner. Even so, our group connected immediately, and soon we were having a festive dinner at the Oasis Restaurant. At the Oasis, Leticia announced that it was safe to eat and drink everything. We could even enjoy the fresh green salad without fear of ingesting hidden parasites. This was certainly not true in Guatemala City, so we all took advantage of the good news and dived into the ample buffet. In addition to salads and fresh vegetables, the buffet offered vegetarian entrees and a variety of chicken dishes. The total bill for each of us was the equivalent of $4.00US, which included dessert and coffee. We were all having such an interesting conversation, that we almost forgot the purpose of our visit. The many explosions of firecrackers outside reminded us of the New Year's celebration, and we quickly joined the huge crowd that was gathered in the town square. For the next two hours, we listened to the music, danced, and just enjoyed ourselves. It was too noisy for conversation, so we leaned into the music and let it lead us. There were fireworks exploding all around.

At about 11:00 PM, I excused myself and went to our hotel. It had been an emotionally tiring day for me, sadly, my last day with the children on the street, for an indeterminate time. Our Antigua hotel was definitely far more commodious than El Hoyo, but it was, at $2.00 per night, well below the level at which any stars could be awarded. The room was damp and the bed was hard, and also clammy with moist coldness. There were no windows. The toilet in the shared bath had no water in it, so it could not be flushed, and had not been for some time. It was probably a good thing that the bathroom light bulb was out and the room was in total darkness.

We were two in a room. Betje and I would share this tiny room. I lay on my back on the cold, damp bed and noticed a slight opening in the curtain that was touching my right hand. I could hear loud music and shouts of celebration so clearly. I pulled aside the curtain a bit and found myself peering down into a huge room that looked to be a banquet hall. There was a sideboard along one wall on which food was laid out. There was a gigantic TV broadcasting New Year's Eve festivities somewhere. In addition, there was a radio with large speakers blasting out Latin music. Incongruously, in the exact center of the banquet hall was parked a blue Volkswagen bus. Across the room was a gigantic table set with festive red cloth mats and lighted candles. I smelled bacon or sausage cooking and heard the voices of the guests as they prepared to gather for the meal. Later, there was a period of only music and quieter conversation. At midnight, there were loud explosions of fireworks right there in the banquet room. The fireworks lasted for about thirty minutes. Meanwhile, almost everyone in our group had returned, and several of us gathered on the stairs outside our room to watch. I was sure that at any minute, the gas tank of the VW would catch fire and blow apart, but it didn't happen. Leticia had missed the indoor performance, as she had stopped to go to midnight New Year's Mass on the way back to the hotel. We all adjourned to our humid, hard beds as soon as the guests departed below. We could hardly keep from laughing loudly enough to be discovered by the kitchen crew as they cleared away the remnants of the party. Where else could we have had such entertainment at any price?

We were so happy to get out in the warm sunshine in the morning. It had been a spectacular celebration, but we were relieved to return to the familiar streets of the City. That night, my last at the Hotel Spring for a while, I showered, and then washed and thoroughly dried clothes at a nearby launderette, packed, read awhile, and went to bed at 6:45. As I drifted off to sleep, I could hear Los Niños de la Calle gathering in the doorway of the building next door. They felt safe near Casa Alianza, and so did I.

Chapter 3
January 1992
The Journey Home

The journey from Guatemala City to Fronteras by bus, and then down the Rio Dulce by motorboat, is complicated and wonderful at the same time. The only variable that separated me from other travelers that day was that I had no idea of my final destination. I was about to hike into an area that was unknown to me, except for the general description that my son Chad had given of the direction and of the beauty of the region. I counted on his Spirit to join my guides as I ventured into the unknown territory, to which I felt drawn and somehow connected. I made a brief stop at one place to ask if the people with whom Chad had worked were there, but they were away for the week, and I left no message. I left the boat when it docked near one of the scenic rock canyons along the river, and I began the long climb via a narrow path that led into the deeply forested land between the river and the sky.

On the morning of the start of my climb into the mountains, I asked my Spirit Guides and Annie and my little angel daughter, April, "Where did you say we were going?"

"Not far," I felt them answer. It is familiar territory to those who are of the Spirit world. It is "just over the horizon and a little way up the road."

I knew the route would just roll out as I walked along. I would follow the path and watch out for detours and any unforeseen dangers. No matter what happened, it would all be part of the plan.

What was the destination? How would I know when I arrived? I would only know because I was being guided. The answers would come as we travelled. I was sure that I was following a path laid out for me at the beginning of time. I didn't want to take a detour that would throw me off course, but there was no need to be anxious. I felt excitement rather than apprehension.

Should I worry about goals, and objectives, and destinations? Of course not! I was not afraid, and I surrendered to the calmness and joy of the moment. I made a decision to trust and take in the incredible sights and sounds and smells of this ancient forest. I wanted to experience the forest and to be, if possible, a participant in village life. I wanted it to happen spontaneously, and not to be something that my western, logical, controlling mind planned in advance. I wanted to be led to a place where I could be part of the life of the village on the residents' terms. I knew the history of Guatemala. I knew people in the city who could have arranged a visit to the mountains for me. I wanted, instead, to be a traveler "without portfolio." I wanted to be as close to arriving "like a plant carried in on a breeze" as possible… with no expectations in any direction.

I heard clattering in the distance. Was it wagons approaching, or was I suddenly in another dimension, hearing the rattling of sabers or the dragging of chains from centuries past? Was I free to go where I wished, or was I on a pre-set course, being held captive and programmed to an unknown destiny? Again, I told myself, it didn't matter. There was no right or wrong answer. Every outcome was to be welcomed for its unique possibilities.

There was a fine mist in the damp air, and a sort of fog rising in the distance. There was the distinct aroma of the tangy smell of wet earth. The path was like a carpet with a luxurious pad. It had grassy spots and soft soil that made footprints when I stepped on them. I walked on, feeling connected with the earth, and saw above me, as I walked, a canopy of graceful, overhanging tree branches. I heard monkeys chattering. Birds sang high in the trees. Occasionally, I saw flashes of brilliant color as they flew from tree to tree.

Ahead there was a shelter, a lean-to that was quite small. It had a rough-hewn wooden bench inside. As I got closer, I saw that the bench was literally a slice of a tree with bark on three sides and one flat upper surface containing rings. I was drawn to this beautiful work of art, and I sat to rest and look around at the beauty of the scene. I didn't know yet why I was there, or what my mission would be. I felt the positive energy around me that is consistently a message from my Spirit Guides that I am moving forward in a positive direction. Ahead, I saw a swiftly flowing creek way below a narrow bridge that was attached to sturdy tree branches with vines far above the ravine. I had a sturdy walking stick in my hand. I started cautiously over the bridge, but I found that I was more agile than I realized, and I could navigate it easily. On the opposite side, I looked down at the roiling water and marveled at my smooth crossing on that precarious span.

The sun peeked out, and the mist began to evaporate a little. I stopped and took it in, thinking, "It is so exceptionally beautiful here!" I knew that there was no hurry, no need to rush. Wherever I was going, it was comforting to be able to walk at such a leisurely pace and to feel that I was a part of this lush landscape. I was filled with peace and quiet joy. I began anticipating the unknown adventure that lay ahead, quietly confident that I could calmly face whatever challenges arose. The whole picture would unfold in perfect timing. I let any thoughts that clung, fly out into the mist. I surrendered to the moment and listened to sounds that can only be discerned when there is silence.

As I ventured further along the path, I suddenly longed for human companionship, and I seemed to see people walking far ahead of me through the forest in a silent procession. These were the forms toward which I walked, but they dissolved in the remaining mist, and I was alone again. The way was straight. Once again, the silence resonated with a concert of whispering vines, singing birds, and calling animals.

I came to a fork in the path, and there was no clear direction. To the right was a thick stand of trees, and to the left, a continuation of the cleared path. I went left, and somehow felt it was the right choice for the moment. The sun was higher now but it was not overly warm. I walked on and didn't feel at all tired. When I stopped, it was because I saw a little stone formation that looked like it was once an altar. There were remnants of branches around it, but it appeared to have been undisturbed for many years. It was an indication, along with the suspension bridge, that not many people have happened onto this area in the past, and maybe not even in the present. Then I heard a distinct whistle, and an answering one as well. My steps stopped, and I looked cautiously around, but I saw nothing except the trees, some flowers, the path, and the silent, gray-blue sky.

I walked on for about five or six miles. Suddenly, without warning, a group of women appeared on the path just ahead of me. They were dressed in the traje tipica of Guatemala and were speaking in their native dialect, which I did not understand. It was my first opportunity to release pride in an accomplishment that I had thought would be the most essential preparation for my visit here. I was suddenly aware that there was to be absolutely no need for my recently acquired proficiency in speaking the Spanish language.

Chapter 4
January 1992
Meeting

I signed to the women that I was a friend. They looked frightened. I laid down my walking stick and my backpack on the ground. I opened my hands in a gesture that I hoped was peaceful. I held my backpack out to them and invited them to look inside. One of them shyly stepped forward and looked at the contents. I reached in, and laid everything out on the ground. There was my bedroll, a tiny flashlight, some matches, a thermos of water, a mosquito net, my cup, plate, utensils, and small cooking pan. There were some tablets for purifying water, a change of clothes, a few home remedies, a knife, toothbrush and some medical supplies. There was also a fetal heart monitor, which I had been told by friends could be useful in the jungle settlements high above the river – and sometimes even lifesaving.

The women looked with interest, chatting among themselves, and then they smiled shyly. They wore their glossy black hair in long plaits down their backs. They moved and spoke quietly, but their dark eyes shone with warmth and trust. Those with babies carried them in colorful woven cloth slings that the mother could move easily from front to back. Toddlers and older children clung to their mothers' skirts and stood slightly behind them, gazing around shyly as I displayed the contents of my pack.

Finally, I put everything back and sat on my haunches on the ground. The women gestured to me and invited me to join them, and we walked on together. We turned and entered the thick jungle growth that I had observed in the distance. We walked for about two hours in a companionable silence. Along the way, they gathered medicinal herbs and various plants that they use for making dyes. They spoke little, but it was apparent that they were extraordinarily connected to each other, and that they were welcoming me although I was a stranger. I felt both encouraged and excited.

I was in the area of the country where Chad had lived and worked for a time, after he graduated from college and before he would begin teaching. Taking a break from the regimented life of study and before he took a job, Chad had gone on a journey by train on a discounted "Amtrak See America" pass across the US to camp in many of the national parks. In his travels, he had met a couple of young men who were off to an adventure near the Caribbean coast of Guatemala. They were part of a small group of volunteers who would help to build a school and medical facility in the rocky mountainside along the Rio Dulce River. The facility would be unique, as it would incorporate the traditional Mayan medical practices, seek to keep alive the crafts and skills of the ancient culture, and provide education in the native language as well as in Spanish. After the rail excursion, Chad extended his "sabbatical" in order to join the others in travelling to Guatemala and helping to begin the exceedingly difficult construction. He undertook the work with great enthusiasm and his keen sense of humor. No matter what the obstacles, he was not discouraged. When the local government received an offer from a company to buy the land that had been designated for the project, they retracted their promise, and gave notice to the volunteers to vacate the land. Chad took it in stride, confident that he and his friends would obtain another site. The months they had spent in preparation were considered by the volunteers not to be a sign of failure, but rather a step toward eventual success. Chad returned to the US, not knowing that he would not be going back. His accident and passing followed. Chad had loved

Remembering to Dance

Guatemala, and I could see why. I felt as if I had moved closer to the land of his Spirit. I wondered if he ever visited Guatemala in his new heavenly incarnation. In response, I felt Chad's presence, and tears of gratitude appeared in my eyes.

As our little group approached a clearing, I smelled cooking fires. Soon we reached the outskirts of their mountain village in the heart of the jungle. There was a great burst of activity as we approached. The men came forward, gesturing wildly and speaking frantically to convey that something terrible had happened. Their spokesman was later introduced to me as Eadrich, one of the village elders. Eadrich presented an imposing figure, tall and ramrod straight, about a head taller than most of the other men of the village. His head bent slightly so that the dark, kind eyes could look directly into those of the person with whom he was speaking. It was apparent that he was loved and respected by everyone.

As the men wailed in great distress, the women received the message that two of the village boys had been kidnapped by the guerrilla army. The villagers had thought they were concealed from the army in this remote area, but someone who had slipped away and traveled through the jungle and up the river to the city had been followed home, and their location was now known.

There are no written birth records or proof of age in the remote villages. Although the army claims that it takes only those who are eighteen years of age or older, it is common for strong-looking boys as young as twelve or thirteen to be taken from their families, never to return.

Once conscripted, the boys are taught to be soldiers, and are often given drugs upon which they become dependent. They are by nature shy and loyal to their family groups and their fellow villagers, but over time they become hardened to the new way of life and are swept up in a sort of "Stockholm syndrome," in which they develop fierce loyalty to their captors.

I never knew at what point the women had explained my presence. Much of the communication was nonverbal, and people seemed to intuitively understand almost everything. I was beckoned into the line of men, women, and children that was walking around the village circle toward the little bark-sided structure that was their place of meeting. We moved into this small chapel and sat on wooden benches, which were larger versions of the little log bench on which I had rested earlier in the day. Two of the men stood up and related the story of the abduction of the boys. The mothers of the boys wept quietly, and the others joined in. A discussion followed as to the futility of pursuit. Any action taken toward tracking and retrieving the boys would result in retaliation of such force by the guerrilla army that it could mean the total annihilation of the village, by murdering every resident and burning it to the ground. Though this was stated in the Q'eqchi language, it was explained to me in Spanish by a tall, strongly built middle-aged man with kind eyes and a wide smile named Sachirhirr, one of the three village catechists who had been trained at the cathedral parish in Guatemala City. As we walked into the chapel, he motioned for me to sit beside him in the front row. Later, he explained to me why the native Mayan dialect and indigenous customs were so cherished by the people of the village.

During the presentation, voices were subdued. It became more like a funeral than a town hall meeting. Prayers were said. These were simple, heartfelt prayers for the safety of the village, for the well-being of the boys. We left the chapel quietly. I was welcomed with signs and murmurs. I was invited to stay in the home of a couple who introduced themselves as Fabio and Sacniek. We were at home with each other right away. Fabio was of average height with a welcoming grin that lit up his dark eyes and his expressive face. His hair was cut short in the customary style of the village. He was dressed in the typical dress of men and boys, blue jeans and an open necked shirt, which his wife had woven of colorful fabric. His hat was of light-colored woven straw. Sacniek wore her dark hair in a long braid down her back, as did every one of the women in the village. She smiled warmly, but shyly, and held out her baby to meet me. The little girl's name was Xmucane. She was about six months old. Her dark eyes turned to look at me, and after studying me solemnly for a moment, she smiled. Her head was covered with a soft cloud of dark hair that curled slightly. She was strong and sturdy, but still delicate in a way.

I sat silently, in gratitude, as my hosts spoke quietly to each other in that simple, large room that was their home. There were two small benches, a sleeping platform, and two hammocks. That was the extent of the furniture. We seemed to know each other already. I think it is the instinctive feeling of trust that our respective Spirit Guides create in making connections for us in the world in which we walk. Sacniek gently handed Xmucane to me, and I held their little daughter in my arms, singing softly to her. She curled up against me and relaxed. I inhaled her sweet aroma of mint and rosemary and mother's milk. I had seen that Annie and April, and my Spirit Guides, were in another bark-sided, thatch-roofed home, a short distance away, doing some angelic therapeutic touch on a little girl whose arms and legs were bent in odd directions. Earlier I had seen the child, whose name was Dacey, lying on a colorful blanket, trying unsuccessfully to move, and making little whimpering sounds. She calmed as they ministered to her. They were joined by the Spirits of her ancestors, who were also healers, and the effect on this tiny child was quite remarkable. Her mother had mixed a paste of soothing herbs and healing roots. As she applied this to the twisted limbs, the little one made what seemed like a soft cooing sound of happiness.

Throughout the village, women were now preparing the evening meal which was, as always, tortillas with some sugar to keep hunger at bay. There was no attempt made to hide the cooking fires, as the danger of the army invading the village was not realistic. The soldiers were off hunting elsewhere for more "recruits."

The village consisted of a large circle of about twenty bark-sided, thatch-roofed huts. The chapel was identical in exterior construction to the houses. Inside the chapel there were rows of benches and an area in front with a simple wooden altar. Any adornments for the space were carried to the little building from the hut of the catechist and his family at the time of any religious services. Nothing was left there permanently, in case roaming animals entered the building.

Each home had one large room in which cooking, sleeping, and every other household activity took place. The cooking area had small stacks of bowls and utensils, and some meager cooking supplies. The sleeping platform was supplemented by a hammock or two.

After dinner, in the dark, everyone lay down to sleep for the night. It was comforting to me to be in the village, and to hear the jungle sounds at somewhat of a distance, as I fell into a deep sleep. I dreamed of walking and singing, and I thought gratefully of my life and gave thanks for every one of its fascinating twists and turns.

I woke to the delicious aroma of tortillas cooking and the sounds of morning rituals. The children brought in water. The men returned with firewood and some fish. I had slept longer than I intended, and no one had objected! I received and exchanged smiles and greetings, which were spoken so softly as to be almost wordless, as I prepared for the day. My new companions moved through the days with grace and a steady rhythm, accomplishing the most difficult tasks smoothly and efficiently. Conversation was minimal, but there was a feeling of energetic confluence – much like the regular motion and beauty of a gently flowing stream.

Sacniek handed me a warm tortilla as I returned from the outdoor latrine and from washing in the stream. She invited me to go with the women and children on an herb-gathering excursion. I quickly assembled a little first-aid kit for my supplies, filled my thermos with water, and off we went. I was wearing a full, lightweight skirt, an embroidered cotton blouse, and hiking shoes. The traditional garments, called huipils, that the women and children wear are colorful, and yet practical. They, of course, were barefoot or in sandals. I thought to myself, "Maybe I will be brave enough for sandals soon!" We spread out from the path to find the most tender shoots and the hidden roots. I knew that Annie and April were with us, but they are able to be in more than one place at a time, so I imagined them also joining the grandmothers as they calmed and encouraged the little girl back in the village.

Suddenly the sky darkened, thunder rolled in, and we were pelted with steady raindrops. We hurried to protect our bolsas, which held the treasures we had gathered, and tried to find a tree large enough to shelter us for a time. It soon became apparent that we were "rained out." Thunder roared, lightning flashed ahead of us, and the rain poured down. We decided to return to the village.

Ahead of us, we heard a mighty crack, and a large tree fell across the path. Some of the little ones were frightened and ran to their mothers or older siblings. We found a way around the fallen tree and began to walk quickly toward the safety of the village. I was grateful for my sturdy hiking boots! The children were undeterred by their lack of footwear. They scampered along the path, splashed through puddles and climbed over rocks and branches with great skill and ease.

Just as we were almost past the fallen tree, one of the children slipped in the mud and I felt against a jagged branch. Her mother screamed and pulled her free of the tangle of leaves and branches and gathered her close. The girl, named Xoc, is a child of strong will and delicate beauty. Her dark hair fell gracefully around her face, and her dark eyes grew large with fear as she watched blood spurt from the wound. I was standing near them and quickly rushed over to Xoc. As the little girl sobbed in fright and in pain, I spoke to her and to her mother softly, and pressed firmly on the tear in her slender leg. Her mother placed her hand over mine, and together we applied pressure until the bleeding subsided, and we were able to dress the wound. We wiped away the mud as best we could with water from my thermos. Xoc's mother let me apply some antibiotic ointment from my first-aid supplies, then a bandage. The other children were incredibly quiet and subdued as we continued to step carefully over the tangled brush.

Reaching home, we found a soggy mess! The houses are constructed for strength and durability, but also are quite open for ventilation. There are spaces in the bark sides for fresh air to pass through. There was no point in trying to dry anything, or to attempt to cook, at the height of a rainstorm! Xoc was given a drink of chamomile tea, and a poultice of herbs was applied to the gash on her leg. She was soon asleep in her mother's arms.

The families gathered in the dark, welcoming chapel, which seemed to be the driest place. Fabio delighted us all with his animated, dramatically performed stories of the origins of the Mayan people. They were told in a lyrical tone, with expressive gestures, about the great forces of nature that participated in the creation and history. Everyone gave their full attention. He brought out his guitar, other men joined in, and we sat and listened to Mayan songs and prayed for sunshine, gentle winds and a bountiful harvest.

I let my thoughts roam far and wide as the words and music flowed through and around me. I contemplated how much I love my life, and that I had such gratitude for the beauty of the families in this village.

I thought about the singlemindedness of people who come together and weave a life of beauty and purpose with extremely limited resources. I thought of their majestic creation story, and of their connection to the earth, the sky, the water sources, the fire, and the air. And I thought of their language. Many people looking at the country from the outside assume that Spanish is the language of the people of Guatemala. I had made that assumption myself. I was now learning that, in actuality, the Spanish are considered to be the conquerors who tried to supplant the ancient Mayan culture. There is a belief by some that it is a "step up" for a subjugated people to learn to speak and read and to be recognized by names in the "new language." It is meant to be a privilege to choose a Spanish name for oneself and one's children. In some geographic areas, it is the law. There is, however, an unspoken understanding, which runs deep within the culture, that the customs and language of the earliest Mayan generations are sacred, and are not to be extinguished. Whether openly or in secret, the indigenous people treasure these traditions and spiritual beliefs, and the Mayan dialects.

I was more than a guest in this sacred space. I was already accepted as part of the village and its people. Once again, the baby fell asleep in my lap. It was such a gift to be able to share this beautiful little one with her family for a few hours. My heart sang.

After the storm subsided, we went to our homes to build cooking fires and to prepare a simple meal, which included a few pieces of the delicious fish caught that morning. We ate to the accompaniment of thunder claps and lightning flashes, but the steady downpour had stopped. We were enfolded in almost total darkness. There were no dry blankets that night! Fortunately, the weather was warm, as we lay wrapped in our semi-dry clothing, serenaded by the thunder.

PART TWO

Chapter 1
October 1995
New Life

Almost four years had passed since I had followed my heart to the village in the mountains. Little had changed during that time in the rhythm of village life. For me, personally, everything had changed. I no longer needed a Spanish-speaking translator. I was an integral part of the village, and I felt interconnected with every one of the men, women, and children in it. I had learned from the best of teachers how to make my own small contribution. I had been taught to plant and to tend the small communal garden plots. I could gather cotton from the plants as it matured, and I was learning the process of preparing and hand-spinning the soft strands. Dyeing was still beyond my field of expertise, though. I could make and cook tortillas, fish, and vegetables. I was learning more each day about gathering medicinal plants from the forest. I was hoping that I could stay here forever.

Each day passed in procession with those that preceded and followed. The seasons made their appearance, as did the phases of the moon. It was a time of continual Thanksgiving for me. There was no frantic race to compete with anyone. Our reason for being was to live together and celebrate life as it came, one day following the next.

Our dear friends and neighbors, Colel and Gabor, would be welcoming their first child in October, just before the seasons changed from winter to summer. I remembered, with tenderness, the marriage of these young people a year earlier. Colel was about fifteen years old at the time, and Gabor was eighteen. Colel was a beautiful young woman of average height, with glossy black hair that she wore in a long braid down her back. Her serious black eyes looked at the world with a sense of wonder, and her lips parted in a friendly smile for young and old alike. Gabor, on the other hand, was a serious young man who was hardworking and had a love of music. His father had trained him as a builder, and together the two men repaired and replaced the little thatch-roofed, bark-sided homes in the village as needed. Gabor had a mop of glossy black hair, strands of which seemed to want to travel in many different directions. He wore the typical straw hat that resembled the headgear of the traditional American cowboy. The woven texture of the straw gave good protection from sun and rain.

It had not been an easy pregnancy, but Colel bore the constant morning sickness and swollen hands and feet without complaint. She was about sixteen years old now, and skilled at weaving. She took up her loom every day, and created exquisite patterns in the cloth that she lovingly produced. Colel had woven a blanket in which to wrap and carry their child. She produced beautiful garments as well, in anticipation of the December market in Guatemala City.

This was the year that many from the village would travel to the market, early in December. It was an ambitious undertaking, which had been planned carefully during the years since my arrival. Thousands of tourists and seasonal residents flock to Guatemala for the summer's drier weather in the months from November to May. Many, many indigenous people take market stalls in the city to sell native crafts and produce of every kind. The December market provides income for some villages that is necessary for survival for the entire year. The women worked steadily in preparation, and the men did also. The men and boys carved many beautiful objects from pieces of wood gathered from the fallen tree branches near the village. They also carved elaborate slingshots. These were formed in the shape of swiftly moving birds and animals with the idea in mind of inspiring a smooth and graceful delivery of the stone, with the help of the Spirit of the animal depicted.

Decorative carvings of saints, as well as mythical figures, were crafted by ancient stone chisel and knife as well. With fingers moving like lightning, the women braided strips of palm fronds and shaped banana leaves by hand to form beautiful platters and bowls. Another of the market favorites is the "straw" cowboy or rancher's hat, woven from palm leaves.

While everyone planned for the upcoming trek and produced something almost every day to add to the growing cache of treasures, Colel dreamed of her child. She wanted her baby to be healthy and strong. She worked valiantly to eat what she could, from the meager supplies, to ensure the health of her baby. Colel was close to the time of delivery. She propelled her swollen body slowly around the village each day, doing her part and contributing to daily chores. Some of the children were always at her side to help her sweep a floor, to grind corn, or to bake tortillas.

Gabor loved his wife's delicate beauty. Her face seemed to him to glow with an inner light. Her long, dark hair framed a round face that always had a smile for him.

If Gabor helped her, he was teased good-naturedly by the other men. He was proud, in his own way, but he was also terrified of the birthing process and didn't want the others to know. He saw the twisted frame of little Dacey daily, and he prayed silently to the Spirits that his son or daughter would be perfect in every way – and that his wife would be able to endure childbirth and survive. Gabor was usually a free spirit who loved to dance and sing and tell jokes. He had become exceptionally quiet in recent weeks, and Colel wondered if he still cared for her, or if maybe he was repulsed by her swollen body and her constant sickness. She wanted this pregnancy to end happily, and to hold their baby in her arms.

Colel had been experiencing somewhat regular, but mild contractions since early that morning. Suddenly, she put down her hand loom and cried out softly in pain. A strong contraction shook her body. Her face turned the color of ashes at this new sensation, and she staggered to her sleeping platform, her hand on her abdomen. She groaned and cried out again.

Marit glided into the little bark-sided hut almost at once. She was the midwife who skillfully attended every birth in the village. Marit's very presence brought a sense of serenity and quiet confidence. She soothed Colel and murmured softly to her, almost singing. Colel quieted and slept fitfully until the next contraction came. It seemed to rip through her, and Marit feared that something was not right. When she sent for me to bring the fetal heart monitor, I was there in a flash. Marit was skeptical of such things, but she was wise and trusting. I listened to the baby's heartbeat and invited Marit to do the same. The baby's heart was strong, but examination showed that she or he was in the breech position. This would not be an easy birth, but together, with patience, and with the prayers and ministrations of the Spirits surrounding us and connecting us, we would succeed in bringing this strong, determined infant into the world of earth dwellers.

Our belief was that because natural, vaginal childbirth was our preference (and in this situation, our only choice), we would have to accept two premises:

1. That the baby had positioned itself in what seemed to it to be the best position.

2. That the mother's position, as she labored to birth the baby, would be determined quite naturally by her body as it adapted to her baby's positioning.

Gabor came into the hut looking terrified. He moved close to Colel, and reached out tentatively to take her hand. Marit immediately included him in the birthing process, and encouraged him to stay near his wife and to be ready to help her move around as much as possible when she woke, and to encourage her to breathe with little panting breaths through each contraction. He still looked scared, but he readily agreed to help, and he was soon engrossed in his role as labor coach.

Chapter 2
October 1995
Love in Action

When the next contraction started, several of us helped Colel to move onto her hands and knees. Marit explained to her that this would help her baby because the baby was in a "sitting position." Marit wanted to give Colel a plant-based remedy to hasten the birthing process, but the other women discussed it with her, and she agreed to wait.

Sacniek, the woman I now considered to be my sister, came in to help, and volunteered to heat some water. She got to work right away, bringing in water and heating it slightly in a clay pot.

Meanwhile, we encouraged Colel to walk around and to stay active, as this would encourage her baby to keep moving along the journey toward birth.

As the contractions grew stronger, Colel dropped to her hands and knees automatically. Marit instructed Gabor to soak a piece of cloth in the warm water, and to apply it to his wife's lower back, which (in the absence of a warm shower) gave her some relief. The women showed her ways to breathe that would be relaxing, and Marit taught her how to move and sway from side to side to bring some comfort.

Within four hours, the contractions were much stronger, and we could see that her cervix was dilated and that the baby's bottom was ready to emerge. We kept Colel moving as much as possible, and kept applying the warm water compresses to her lower back. Marit and Sacniek spoke softly to her, encouraging her and calling on the Spirits to help both parents to stay hopeful and positive as their baby prepared to emerge into the world.

After another hour had passed, Colel began to feel the urge to push. I fashioned a makeshift pillow by folding a piece of cloth over a blanket, and when Colel could no longer hold up her entire weight on her hands and knees, Gabor sat facing her, and she rested the front of her body and her head on the pillow that lay in his lap. He continued to speak softly, almost musically, to her, and to breathe with her through each contraction. She was shaking from the unusual muscle activity, but she was giving the birthing process her entire attention and was excited as each new level was reached.

Colel felt her baby emerging and cried out loudly.

"Push, Push," we encouraged in Q'eqchi', and she did. She felt the baby's bottom suddenly slip out. She cried with joy this time, and then found herself caught up in another powerful contraction, and made an enormous effort to push again. This time it was the little girl's legs, arms and upper body that slid through into Marit's gentle hands. Marit checked the placenta and it was fine, not tangled or constricted in any way. One additional huge push, and Colel's and Gabor's daughter's head emerged. We heard a strong cry, and soon Colel was lying face up on the pillow, and her strong, perfectly formed infant was placed at her breast.

Tears streamed down Colel's and Gabor's faces. They were ecstatic. Gabor lay beside his wife and daughter on the sleeping mat as she examined each tiny finger and toe and stroked the fine, black hair that framed their daughter's face.

Once the afterbirth was delivered and the umbilical cord was cut, Colel and the baby were bathed and the baby was wrapped in a blanket. There was no longer any doubt in Colel's mind that Gabor loved her.

The baby was a delight to all. Her mother recovered surprisingly rapidly, and after the traditional period of rest after delivery, Colel joined the other women at the stream once more as they scrubbed and washed their clothes, then spread them out on the rocks to dry in the sunshine. The baby lay quiet and happy, wrapped snugly in her colorful blanket on Colel's back. She looked out of her wrappings with wise eyes. Surely that was a smile on her lips!

Chapter 3
November 1995
Advent Journey

It was the village custom to wait for one month before naming the baby. The infant mortality rate was extremely high, and it was believed that it was not right to name a child too soon, because if the baby died, that name would always be associated with sorrow and loss and probably would not be used by others.

As the weeks passed, days were getting warmer, and the sun smiled down as each of us worked. One day we watched a flock of colorful birds gliding in to settle in the trees. The mating season was at hand!

The villagers held dances in tribute to those who had slipped away to the Spirit world, as well as the new arrivals, and we celebrated the village children born that year. In a sacred naming ceremony, Colel's and Gabor's baby received the name of Xena, which means "honored guest."

Every year at this time, we mourned the loss of the two young boys whose fate we might never know. Their lives were also celebrated in a spirited dance. And every day the store of treasure that would be taken to the market grew in size and in splendor. The men hunted and brought back a small ration of game to be skinned and prepared for drying. Fish were caught and dried also. Soil was prepared for planting an early crop of squash and corn that would germinate and begin to grow while we were away. A larger planting of beans, corn, squash, and root vegetables would be planted in the months after our return, to take advantage of the rainy season.

Eight people would stay behind to take care of the village, the crops, and the chickens. Among them was a frail, elderly man who could no longer travel. Three others were Dacey and her parents. Dacey was now almost six years old. She was almost pain free, due to the ministrations of the healers and the compresses of herbs that her mother applied several times daily. She was able to speak a few words and had begun to smile occasionally. The others who would stay were two couples who had volunteered to help with tending the crops, doing the daily village chores, and fishing.

Those who remained would be the caretakers while we travelled. There would be six weeks of travelling and selling in the city before we would return home. The people of the village would live in a temporary camp near the shanty towns on the outskirts of the city. I would stay at the Hotel Spring in the city so that I, as a gringo, would not call attention to them. I would be at the market every day along with the crowds from all over the country. There would be someone left at the campsite each day to guard the villagers' meager possessions. We all hoped that everyone would remain in good health and be able to perform their daily tasks so that the risky enterprise of relocating and selling at the market would succeed.

It was during this period of preparation that I made my daily visits to the cave, and prayed for guidance for the journey ahead. Returning assured that all would be all right no matter what occurred, I prepared with my village family for the journey.

On a cloudy morning in late November, we gathered in a procession, walking two abreast, and forty-two of us, men, women, and children – along with many of our Spirit Guides – started out on the journey to the market. There would be a ten-day walk to our destination. The men and women carried packs laden with items to be sold, as well as packs of food and water. Animals and vehicles were not part of this trek. It was not even a consideration. Such luxuries were out of the question. All of the villagers were used to travelling on foot.

The dry season had begun, and we hoped that there would be no unexpected heavy showers. The well-established pattern involved steady walking for three full days, followed by an afternoon of rest to wash our clothing and ourselves in a stream. Once we reached the river, there were friends who transported the group across. We traded a few items for this service, and for some additional food to carry along for the journey. The next phase of travel was on foot, along the winding mountain highways.

La Ruidosa marked the "almost halfway point." There is a gas station with the luxury of hot and cold running water, located along the highway in La Ruidosa. I was useful here, masquerading as "the tourist." I, the pale-skinned gringo who looked like a possible person with money, was able to collect several containers full of hot and cold water.

We found a spot, a distance off the road in a grove of trees, where we could camp and bathe and wash clothing with this luxurious gift of water. The children played and practiced bird calls while the adults enjoyed the rest and relaxation. Just before dawn, the procession began again, walking with renewed energy toward the now not-quite-so-distant goal, and with full water containers. As the sun appeared and rose higher, our clothes dried as we walked. I was thinking that had I been in this beautiful and mysterious land as a tourist, I would have been focused on where to change money, where to get a bus, where to buy a meal, where to find a hotel room. It would have been rush, rush, rush with no time to think or to dream. In the rhythm of the walking, and the hush of those around me, I could hear each bird song, notice every rock and tree, and feel completely relaxed and happy in the company of my companions.

I loved taking my turn carrying babies and guiding young children. There were none of the complaints and none of the distress that one would have expected from children raised in the culture from which I came. These were families at peace within themselves, with their surroundings, and with each other. There was such strength in their harmony.

On the morning of the tenth day, we arrived at the clearing in the trees near a rutted dirt path, not far from a garbage dump, that would be our campground. The distance to the market would be only five miles each way. That seemed to me, in perspective, borrowing a metaphor from my past experience, like a walk to the mailbox. While the rest of the group set up the camp, I walked into the city and found the Hostel where I had booked and paid in full for a room way in advance. The coffee aroma drifted in from the modest dining area. I merely smiled and let it permeate my senses. I carried no money or credit cards. My intention, as always when I travel on these adventures, and at other times too, is to experience with accuracy the lives of the friends whom I meet and with whom I travel. I would wait to eat tortillas and drink fresh water with my companions the next morning at the market.

Sleep came quickly, but it felt strange to be on the lumpy mattress instead of being rolled in a colorful blanket, resting on the grass, and being surrounded by many friends near me and sheltered from above by the canopy of stars.

I dressed quickly in the morning, leaving nothing behind. We were to meet at the market and set up our stall.

Chapter 4
December 1995
The Market

La Terminal, (the enormous market in Zone 4 of Guatemala City) covers a distance of six extraordinarily large city blocks in all directions. It is the place where hotels and restaurants buy their daily produce. It is vast, and it is incredibly crowded and busy.

Our group of stalls was in the area toward the center of the complicated expanse. Fortunately, they were in an area that was surrounded by food vendors. That feature would hopefully be a means of attracting customers. The villagers had a contact in the city, who for a modest fee had arranged for the use of the stalls for a period of two weeks. He had, as part of the agreement, brought in some precious commodities in the form of rough-hewn wooden tables so that the merchandise could be displayed at a convenient level. On two of these tables, small racks, made from pairs of dowels inserted into wood bases and connected with wires, displayed jewelry and other small hanging objects. Woven garments and blankets lay across slightly elevated crates and boxes, and also hung around the sides of the stands.

The villagers quickly made trades for any materials that they needed so that they could spend each day in producing more items for sale. They continued carving, as well as weaving on hand looms, throughout each day. The market rapidly filled as the sun began to rise. The delicious smells of food, and of coffee, permeated the cool morning air. The displays of glistening fruits and vegetables of all colors and shapes, the racks of hanging meat, the overflowing baskets of fresh fish and the calls of vendors promoting their wares filled the enormous space, bringing a feeling of intimacy among all who gathered here with hopes and dreams of success. The excitement was contagious, and our hopes soared.

Many of the stalls were managed by children of only seven or eight years of age as the adults spread out and carried samples of their merchandise throughout the market. The children of our village were not experienced in city life, so the parents kept them close and trained them in displaying the items for sale. They also put down a blanket on the floor behind the display tables so that the younger children would have a safe place to play. I worked as a runner, going out on errands to obtain needed items. In between, I played with the little ones, and we also did exercises to move our arms and legs within the safety of the space.

I could sense our Spirit Guides, and had a feeling of peace as well as anticipation that all would be well. Sales were off to an excellent start. The adults took turns walking through the market with various items draped across their arms and hands. We traded for food in small quantities, and each of us had a tortilla. One of the women at a stall near us brought a gift of a substantial meal for the children on the first day, and she continued to do so each day that we were at the market.

The three village catechists attended a study group at the Diocesan Center in the City before joining the others at the Market. They came back to us inspired, enthusiastic, and eager to hold an open-air worship service under the stars.

At the beginning of our second week at the market, we all joined in the solemn vigil at the campground on the eve of the fourth Sunday of Advent. The liturgy, as was the custom, combined ancient Mayan worship practices with a form of Roman Catholicism. In their ancient language, the catechists led the reading and all joined in reciting the Magnificat, a tribute to the Spirit of the Mother.

My soul proclaims the greatness of the Lord
My spirit rejoices in God my Savior
For he has looked with favor on his lowly Servant.
From this day, all generations will call me blessed.
The almighty has done great things for me
And holy is his name.
He has shown mercy to those who reverence him
In every generation.
He has shown the strength of his arm.
He has scattered the prideful in their conceit.
He has cast down the almighty from their thrones
And lifted up the lowly.
He has filled the hungry with good things
And the rich he has sent away empty.

Several of the villagers offered prayers in the Mayan language, and the service concluded with the Lord's Prayer.

Warmed by the prayers and grateful for the thus-far-successful market, the little group went to their sleeping mats, and I walked back to the Spring Hotel.

Early the next morning, I returned to the camp, and as we greeted the first streaks of light in the sky, we walked silently and reverently to the market for another day of selling and bargaining.

By 8 AM, the market was bustling. The children stayed close to their parents and siblings, as instructed. Each was looking forward to a breakfast tortilla with a bit of fish and a drink of water. Suddenly, as the crowds grew and walking became difficult, there was a disturbance and something that sounded like a gunshot. A few small, ragged children who were not from our village scurried away from in front of our stall. They left behind a taller boy of about ten, who was lighting a large firecracker. Everyone fixed their eyes on him, and some of the men moved toward him to try to stop the explosion. As he ran and escaped the confusion, with his pursuers on his heels, no one noticed the other two tall, slender youths who moved in from behind and quickly grabbed baby Xena from her sleeping mat, and also deftly captured a five-year-old girl named Zahra, the daughter of a young couple named Sachirhiro and Itzel, before she could make a sound.

How could this be? While Colel was taking a turn at the counter, she had left a sixteen-year-old girl in charge of her baby, who was lying happily on the play blanket. The teenager had been drawn to the excitement around the firecracker and had told little Zahra to "watch Xena for only one moment."

It actually happened so fast that nothing could have been done to prevent it. Zahra and Xena simply vanished. Returning from the counter merely a few feet away, Colel searched frantically, tears running down her cheeks; then she screamed, and was immediately surrounded by the others. They fanned out and searched quickly, but everyone knew what had happened. It was their worst nightmare!

Thousands of homeless children live on the streets of Guatemala City. They have been abandoned for many reasons. From quite early ages they learn survival tactics, and many take jobs such as prostitutes, beggars, drug sellers, and thieves. Most sniff glue to dull the pain of hunger and of life in general. Some join gangs, others work for individuals who provide them with a small, bare room in which many sleep at night, along with glue to sniff. At that time, there was a huge illegal market for the sale of babies for adoption.

The babies were called "orphans," and were usually sold to wealthy American and European couples who actually believed them to be orphans. The younger the baby, the more readily marketable he or she was. Acquiring the infants required stealth and speed. Taking infants and small children from distracted parents at the market was considered to be an easy task by the perpetrators. The families did not have the financial resources needed for pursuit. The stakes were high.

The diversion that day had been created to give the experienced young abductors a chance to move in and take the two children. They had disappeared without a trace in about ten seconds. Looking further without a plan would be futile. I ran rapidly through my mental Rolodex of contacts and possible solutions. I knew of only one course of action to take, and it involved a huge risk.

Chapter 5
December 1995
Posada

Immediately after the tragic kidnapping at the market, I spoke with Eadrich and said that I would like to volunteer to help Colel and Gabor locate Xena, and to reunite them as quickly as possible. All of the men and women of the village had gathered around us as we spoke.

Of course, I would volunteer to do the same for Sachirhiro and Itzel, Zahra's parents, but together we decided upon two separate rescue plans due to the age and the likely locations of the two girls. My suggestion was that I work through contacts that I had through the Sanctuary Movement in the United States, who would lead me in a safe direction in Guatemala. I would go without delay to begin the search, and I would return to the market with a report as quickly as I could. Everyone nodded and thanked me, and several volunteered to go with me, but it was decided that it would be safer for the missing children if I went alone and they stayed on site at the market.

I walked toward the center of the city, found a public telephone, and placed a long-distance call to my friends Chris and Arnie Miller, who lived quietly in the beautifully planned community of Crofton, Maryland. In the somewhat exclusive and protective confines of this Washington, DC suburb, they were raising their three young daughters, Sarah, Jennifer, and Susan. Chris taught reading to gifted students at the newly renovated Crofton Elementary School, and Arnie was a lawyer practicing in a large DC firm with a satellite office in Tacoma, Maryland, near several churches that offered sanctuary to people escaping violence in their home countries. Fortunately, the timing was good. Chris would be on Christmas break and would probably be at home when I called.

I breathed a sigh of relief when I heard Chris's voice. I began with a pre-arranged coded message, which got her immediate attention. As we discussed birthday parties and other innocuous subjects on the brief call, the message came across that Arnie would act upon the minute the call ended. I knew I had completed the first step of the plan, because Arnie would call the lawyer who would be helping me in Guatemala.

I walked quickly into the city and stopped at the photo shop that developed film on premises, asking that my roll of film be developed through the "one-hour photo service." I then went to the office of the lawyer whom I knew to be directly connected to the Sanctuary networks. I stood anxiously for a few minutes in his waiting room, and then he saw me at once. He had already heard from Arnie Miller in Maryland. He was expecting me, and he was prepared to assist in any way possible. I would first try to locate the infant, Xena, as she was in immediate danger of being sold illegally to one of the underworld groups that brokered illegal adoptions. The lawyer and I agreed not to meet in person again, as there was careful surveillance of foreigners by the police. We didn't want to arouse suspicion.

Funds immediately became available through the sanctuary network, that could be used to purchase the baby directly, once she was located, and before she was passed along the chain of nefarious dealers. At that point, Gabor and Colel and Xena would be given travel documents, with fees for safe transport over the border into and through Mexico to the United States toward a prearranged safe haven.

The lawyer and I agreed that I would contact him with a coded message as soon as I had information as to Xena's whereabouts. By then I would have the photo print that would identify her. I would call the lawyer with the coded message, then a courier would come to my hotel to pick up the photo and the address where she could be found.

I was too deeply involved in carrying out these critical steps to feel anxious or even concerned. I imagined going into the spiritual mode of designing the pattern of the tapestry that would be woven step by step, row by row, until a resolution would be revealed. I surrendered to this familiar process of being prayerfully led through the steps that would open and create the pathways that would take me to the best possible outcome.

I walked next to the place where I hoped Leticia would be reading to the children of the street. I also hoped she would recognize me. It had been four years since we had seen each other. My hair had grown long and was now hanging down in a somewhat straggly ponytail. My skin had been baked in the sun to a very light tan color. I found her alone, between groups, and we walked together for a short distance in the opposite direction from where she was working. Leticia and I were overjoyed to see each other again, but even as we hugged, she could see that I had something urgent and serious to tell her. I told her only that I needed to verify whether an infant matching Xena's description had been taken in the past few hours to the place in Zone 2 where we both knew that similar "orphans" were often temporarily housed. Letitia could do this without drawing attention, as she knew people who worked there and she often casually dropped by the place. She would check immediately and contact me later at the hotel. She told me that, sadly, the kidnapping problem was increasing. We promised to get together, if possible, while I was in the City, and then we went our separate ways.

I looped around and headed toward the market after picking up the photos. At the market, I met with my village family, and it was decided that Colel and Gabor would be prepared to leave with me the next time I returned. At that time, I would, hopefully, be bringing the news that their daughter had been rescued by friends in the Sanctuary network. We all discussed the other plan to rescue Zahra. We prayed together, led by the catechists, and I went back toward the hotel.

When I reached the Hotel Spring, I found that a message had just arrived from Leticia. It contained only one word. "Si." I immediately went out, found a public telephone, and called the office of the lawyer to provide the agreed-upon code, "Please tell Señor that his two pairs of shoes are ready to be picked up." Then I sat down to wait.

The Hotel Spring is normally one of my favorite places in the world. It is a no-frills hotel where young people and budget travelers from all over the world congregate. It is on the order of a well-run youth hostel. It has a picturesque dining area, and it serves an excellent and inexpensive breakfast. The rooms are small, simple, and clean, with shared baths and hot-and-cold running water that works!

The contact came early that afternoon, as I sat inhaling the scent and longing for a strong cup of coffee. A student brushed past and slipped me a card. This was the moment! I set aside any doubts and gave thanks for this rapid response. The card contained the name of the lawyer with whom I had met earlier that day.

I passed the small packet to the courier that contained the photo of Xena that had been developed. I had written her name and the words "Zona 2" on the back, confirming the location of the "orphanage." I included the number of Gabor and Colel's stall at the market.

Everyone was prepared to leave the market quickly as soon as the next contact was made. Meanwhile, the lawyer in

Guatemala City quickly made the deal to purchase Xena from the "orphanage" where she was lying, along with other infants, in one of the iron cribs with high sidebars. The lawyer had her safely transported to his office, where he prepared travel documents for the family. The courier returned to the hotel coffee shop to give me a packet of instructions, then quickly disappeared. Included in the packet was the cash I had arranged for while I was at the law office that morning. I had prepared a personal check, which would be sent to Arnie Miller. Arnie would reimburse the lawyer in Guatemala, who had advanced cash to me, both in quetzals and in US dollars, so that I could move more rapidly in searching for Zahra.

I took a taxi to the market, quickly explained to an incredulous Gabor and Colel what was about to happen, promised everyone else that I would return later to the campsite, found another cab, and went with them (insisting on silence during the ride for their protection) to the law office. I pointed them toward the elevator and had to trust that they would arrive safely at the right office. It was so hard for all of us to not be able to say one last goodbye. I walked from there to a public phone and called the law office to make sure that all was well. I was assured that everything was going according to plan and that parents and child had been reunited. It was a beautiful moment. I smiled and gave thanks to my Spirit Guides, my loved ones in Spirit and to Divine Source. The tapestry was being revealed bit by bit, the weave was perfect, and the colors were magnificent. I walked in the waning evening light to the campsite where the villagers would have gone to spend the night.

At the campsite, the villagers finally consented to take the bus back to the river rather than walking. They would have to be back at home quickly in order to be there when Zahra was returned. It was with some difficulty that we finally agreed that

I was to be honored, as a member of the village family, with the opportunity to provide the bus fare for this journey.

We discussed the details of the plan for rescuing Zahra, whom we now knew was to be taken the next day to a place on the river called Casa de Esperanza. Her young male cousins were designated as the ones to meet me there at the port, on the day after Christmas, with the expectation of taking her across the river toward their village in a borrowed canoe. The village leaders would wait in a concealed area on the other side of the river to meet the canoe and to guide the young men and Zahra up into the mountains and safely home. That part of the tapestry was still to be woven.

I had made arrangements to meet people from Casa de Esperanza the next day, midway between the city and the river. I was sent off with a prayer and a blessing from my beloved family members. I would not be able to return to the village or to the river in the immediate future. Our love for each other would always connect us. We said goodbye with an abundance of both smiles and tears. I left copies of the photos and the bus fare with Eadrich and walked back to the hotel, humming softly and hopefully.

Meanwhile, Gabor and Colel received their travel papers. With their meager belongings, they would make their own posada, as had Mary, Joseph, and their infant in the biblical account, seeking a safe haven and a new home in a strange country, far from the political turmoil of their homeland.

Chapter 6
December 1995
Hiding in Plain Sight

With the situation well in hand in bringing Xena to safety, I was open to the challenge of locating Zahra and returning her to her parents. I knew that once I took the first step, I was guaranteeing that I, myself, could not return to the village in the mountains that had become my home. Hopefully, with time, those who were illegally holding Zahra would forget her. She would not have been noticed yet as an individual. There was so much activity around the Christmas holiday that the focus would be on fundraising from visitors, and not upon the most recent acquisition by the facility. Still, I could not take a chance, even in the future, of endangering anyone involved.

My greatest challenge lay ahead. At age five, Zahra was beyond what was considered the optimal age for adoption, and it was almost guaranteed that she would be sent to the settlement between Fronteras and Belize for older "orphans," which was a veritable goldmine for donations that were allegedly used to "educate and feed the abandoned children of Guatemala." This was an area in which I could be useful, based on my own training in this work and on my knowledge of the geographic area. I knew I must quickly build a network of support that would allow us to return five-year-old Zahra to her parents and to her own village.

With my Spirit Guides encouraging and protecting me, I quietly reached out to the few people I knew who could lend moral support, and together we formulated a plan. I was to leave immediately for the river, posing as an American tourist who had connections to US churches, and to individuals in Florida who were willing to make substantial donations to help families in Guatemala following the uprisings and wrenching relocations of the 1980s and 1990s. Word went out that the well-connected American woman would tour the areas of Guatemala in which orphans and abandoned children were being cared for. I would send word back somehow if I found Zahra.

One of the main entrepreneurs and opportunists who had risen to power over such an enterprise was known as "Don Alfredo." His wife, Josefina, lived on site most of the year and made the constant appeals for funds that resulted in a steady flow of cash donations. Josefina had developed an additional business venture on the side in which young girls at the "Refugio," when found to be pregnant, were forced to give up their babies for adoption. My friends had told me that recently one of the young, pregnant girls had escaped temporarily. Though she was skillful in hiding in the jungle, she was hunted down with dogs, captured, and taken back to fulfill her "destiny" in producing another child for the adoption scheme.

The children, and the volunteers who cared for them, were kept on a subsistence diet of beans and tortillas, though donors regularly sent large amounts of money for food. The little ones were energetic and outgoing, and made a great impression on tourists. Frequent dockings of river cruise ships insured a ready supply of immediate cash and added names to the list of donors.

College-age volunteers could sign on for Guatemalan adventures that claimed to support a good cause by applying to visit the camp for periods of time, for which they paid several hundred dollars per week. In return, they were put in full charge of the groups of children. It was the job of volunteers to see that the children were dressed, fed, their clothes washed, any medical needs met, disciplined when necessary, put to bed in the evening, and watched through the night. The "rest time" for volunteers came when the children attended school. The school program was conducted in Spanish, and it emphasized quiet attention by all age groups to the one teacher. The children were lined up to sit on benches in order of age. The method of instruction was to have all the children repeat what the teacher said. School was in session for three hours each day.

This was not a place I looked forward to visiting. Before leaving the city, I spent a couple hours at the street markets buying items that would change my appearance to that of a gringo tourist. I bought a used suitcase and filled it with the type of cheap toys that tourists typically donate to village children at Christmas. I did add some practical gifts such as socks and underwear. I selected a few picture books that told stories of Mayan villages (though they were written in Spanish).

Dressed in jeans, and a T-shirt that pictured a scene from Niagara Falls, I added a cap with a visor that proclaimed the wearer to be a member of the American Automobile Association.

Shouldering my backpack and pulling the suitcase along behind me, I did a quick spiritual check-in and looked within myself for the love upon which I would need to stay focused as I ventured into this dark and dangerous place. From Divine Source, I told myself, comes only love. Love of all things and of all people will bring light where there seems to be only darkness and despair.

As I walked toward the bus station. I was calm, protected, peaceful, and filled with hope. I was ready for Christmas.

Chapter 7
Christmas 1995

In the interest of time, I was back to using small amounts of money and all of the dubious advantages of my ethnicity to move or to climb the necessary mountains. The first bus took us four hours out of the City toward the River. Following the directions given to me, I took my backpack and suitcase and stood at an isolated rural bus stop. A man suddenly appeared. He asked if I was going to Casa de la Esperanza. At first, I froze in fear that I had been identified, but I soon relaxed and smiled. I saw that he was not alone. With him were several men and women who were introduced as past or present volunteers at the Casa. This was definitely the "ride" that I had been instructed to meet. I was introduced to a doctor of Bahamian and Welsh descent named Elin, a tall, stately woman in her mid-thirties with ebony skin tones and a serene demeanor, who explained that she was volunteering at a nearby village for a period of several months.

There was also a couple in their late twenties who were interested in being part of the proposed project on which my son Chad had briefly worked. The man, named Allan was a skilled carpenter. A wide, wide, friendly smile peeked from within a bushy brown beard. His eyes were kind and signaled patience and a reservoir of quiet strength. His spouse Naomi, a talented weaver, resembled the legendary image of a woodland sprite. Naomi had been interested in finding a location where she could assist native women in forming a textile co-op. They were both free spirits who traveled around the world teaching, learning, and serving as needed. We were a most compatible group. Some of us were guided into the back of a pickup truck with our luggage. Allan and Naomi sat in the front seat of the pickup with Ed. Our driver, Ed, was the young graduate student from the States who was negotiating for a location on the river where he and others could establish an indigenous, Mayan-run hospital and school whose curriculum would include Mayan history and crafts. The clinic would blend native medicinal remedies with some western practices. Ed's tall stature and powerful frame were somehow completely in tune with his calm demeanor and quiet sense of humor. He could have been wearing a name badge that identified him with the title of Natural Leader, but that was totally unnecessary. I could see why my son, Chad, had been so favorably impressed by this strong, yet gentle, man. He was working temporarily at Casa de la Esperanza, where he kept plans for this project "under the radar." Of course, this was not a subject that I would broach. I was being accepted as a visitor to the project as an American tourist connected with a wealthy parish church in southeastern Florida. This fact limited our conversation to generalities. The others were along to shop at the local regional market and to help load and unload the supplies.

A half hour later, we stopped at a large outdoor market and piled out. The truck transmission had begun slipping, but so far it was functional. I fleetingly thought of the missed opportunity to continue by bus!

The market was large, colorful, and bustling. It was redolent with the delicious scents of tamales and tortillas cooking, and with the tantalizing spices simmering in a pot of chicken soup.

The men hoisted a huge bag of about fifty or sixty cabbages and a tall stack of banana leaves (for making tamales) onto the bed of the truck, as well as restaurant-sized bags of flour, corn meal, sugar, and other supplies. From my assigned seat in the bed of the truck, I could no longer see over the apex of the bountiful cargo to view my fellow passengers. I focused on sending positive energy to the laboring transmission, and on gratitude for this enthusiastic group of volunteers.

Any holiday visitors to the "refuge" would witness no food shortage for the occupants! The children and the volunteers would be well fed, at least for the next ten days. A serious mechanical problem soon had the truck in its grip. With help from those other than me (all those who were not totally surrounded by cabbage, etc.) pushing the truck, the driver got it in reverse and everyone cheered as it ground slowly into first, second, third, and finally fourth gear. We didn't dare attempt any more stops, so we drove straight to the dock near the Casa. A motorboat was waiting for us. We had stopped at Fronteras to buy candy for the piñata that would be launched that evening. We reached the Casa at Livingston at dusk.

Josefina immediately appeared. Her slight, wiry frame was overpowered by her sharp black eyes and her shrill voice. She did not acknowledge the visitors or waste a moment on pleasantries. She just rapidly shouted out orders. She brusquely ordered Ed that he must turn around and navigate the river once more, and then drive immediately back to Guatemala City (over 200 miles each way in the dark on rough roads). She insisted that he should take the truck with the broken transmission. The transmission was by then hanging down under the truck onto the parking area, where we had left it before boarding the boat.

Ed explained to Josefina, in his gentle but firm way, that this would not be wise, though he was careful not to refuse. He persuaded her that he should drive the car instead. She reluctantly agreed. We unloaded the boat, and at about 9:00 PM, Ed left to go back to the City. One of the volunteers rode with him, for which we were all relieved. What was the urgency that required this wildly irrational errand? Josefina wanted Ed to pick up and bring back some Christmas gifts that had been stored at the Orphanage in Zona 2. She said it was an emergency because one of her major donors had not come through with expected gifts, and visitors were due to arrive within the next two days. She must have a number of gifts in evidence for them to see. It was apparent that donations had been received for that purpose, but that no one had followed through to use the money for the purpose which the donors had designated.

Supper was long over, the children were asleep, so after we had unpacked the boat, we got ready to settle in for the night. It turned out that this was an unusual night. In preparation for some special Christmas festivities, a pig was to be slaughtered. The generator was left on all night for this purpose, instead of being turned off at 9:00 PM which would have plunged the area into total darkness.

In the midst of the thick jungle growth, darkness was absolute. A circle of activity had formed in the small clearing beside the building that was described to me as the "teacher's house." The generator-powered lights that were strung across the clearing illuminated the group of exuberant men who were drinking a potent, home-brewed beer, playing musical instruments, and singing loudly. A huge pig was tied to a nearby tree, squealing frantically without pause.

I was assigned to temporary living quarters in the teacher's house, as she was on vacation. The little bark-sided, thatch-roofed hut was, like the other buildings, raised on stilts to prevent flooding in the rainy season in this low-lying area near the river. The roof housed many insects, as well as birds and bats. Inside, I found a bed with a damp mattress and a host of mosquitoes buzzing about. The village was built on a swamp, so dampness was to be expected. It was humid all year round, and bedding was hung outdoors on clotheslines during the day. The air was so thick with moisture that little or no drying took place. All of the mattresses on which the children slept were mildewed.

I removed the sheet from the bed and shook it outdoors. As it swirled back over the mattress, insects immediately dropped from the ceiling to cover it. I was grateful that I had a small blanket and my mosquito net. And so it was that two days before Christmas, I fell into a restless sleep, punctuated by the gentle flutter of bat wings over my head and the eerie squeals of the unfortunate pig. Guitars strummed, and monkeys screamed in the night. The contrast between this place and the peaceful village in the mountains couldn't be greater. In my troubled dreams, I saw Zahra frantically reaching out to me, but the gleaming machete blade of the pig slayer swiped at me whenever I tried to connect with her.

Suddenly, there was a bloodcurdling series of squeals; the men howled and laughed and began a frenzied dance. The pig thudded to the ground in a violent series a series of paroxysms that caused great laughter among the captors. Then there were the clear sounds of butchering. Suddenly, all was quiet.

Ironically, there is almost no meat served at the complex, but at Christmas, as tourists arrive for a look, there is finally permission to kill a pig, and tamales are served for a week. These are enthusiastically assembled by the village women and stuffed with pork and cornmeal.

I was warmly received by a subdued and quite charming Josefina in the morning and given a personal tour of the premises. She gave a detailed account of projects she was working to complete, along with the amounts of money required to finish the work. A donor had recently provided a sizable sum for the construction of additional pigpens. Raising pigs was her favorite project.

One of the volunteers later told me that the children, even the six- to eight-year-olds, had been working for a couple weeks prior to my visit, from sunrise until after dark, on clearing debris, following the collapse of the girls' and the small children's living quarters. The pilings underneath the floor had rotted away. Most of the beds were destroyed when the floor fell in. All of the substructure had to be replaced. Everyone carried bags of cement and hauled concrete blocks from the dock to the site. They worked frantically for weeks to prepare for the Christmas visitors. The food rations were meager: a portion of rice and beans every day. My heart was breaking for all of the captives. I wanted to free them, but I had to realize that I would put everyone in danger with such well-intentioned but grandiose ideas. My task was to gain the trust of Josefina and to return Zahra to her family.

In the dining hall, I saw her. Zahra was wide-eyed and frightened, being herded to a table with other children. I wanted to run to her and take her in my arms. It was with a great effort of will that I left her in the care of her Spirit Guides and mine, along with the enormously capable volunteers, and went back out with Josefina to look at the hydroponic gardens. The lush contents of the greenhouse had been the result of a grant from a European government. However, the beautiful produce was being sold rather than being shared with the residents.

I had seen Zahra, and it was now imperative for me to get word to the friends in the City who were waiting for confirmation. I accepted an invitation from the gardener for a ride in the motorboat to the nearby town of Fronteras, where I found a telephone and relayed the message. The stated purpose of the trip to Fronteras was for me to buy a blanket, as the nights were cool. The small additional blanket that I purchased was colorful and warm.

The gardener confided to me that he had computed the cost of feeding the ever-growing number of pigs, which were also exclusively for sale rather than for on-premises consumption. He said that he had become so concerned that he actually confronted Josefina. She flew into a rage and told him NEVER to speak to her of such things again. His job, he was told, was to follow her orders and not to question them.

That night was Christmas Eve. I knew that I must endure two more nights in this place before the plan to rescue Zahra went into effect. Whether or not the plan succeeded, I must be at the airport and on the plane on the twenty-seventh. It would not be safe for me to stay longer.

When we returned from Fronteras, the gardener introduced me to one of the international volunteers from Germany, whose name was Gerda. She was a tall, blonde-haired, blue-eyed woman in her late twenties, who was visiting from her home country, for six months, as a volunteer. She was fluent in Spanish and was studying in Germany to be a lawyer in the field of international relations. She and I bonded quickly, and she freely answered my questions about the Casa and the programs that were in operation there.

I took a short walk with Gerda. It was a welcome break, and it proved to be extremely interesting to be updated on her studies in Germany as well as her experiences in Guatemala. She and I spent the rest of the morning wrapping gifts for the party that was to be held that night. I longed to join the children and the volunteers in decorating the dining hall, but I could not risk being seen by Zahra.

Suddenly, early in the afternoon, the atmosphere changed, and tension filled the air. I was told that this was a regular occurrence. Josefina had had a furious argument with some of the villagers. As a result, the village marimba band that was to perform at the Christmas Eve festivities had refused to show up. Josefina, who was prone to mood swings, retaliated by deciding that no apples or grapes would be given to the villagers that night, and that she would hold back the gifts that had been wrapped and would not distribute them until the next day. She went to bed, leaving instructions for Ed to send everyone home early and to turn off the generator by 10 PM.

The villagers assembled and devised their own entertainment. They played tape recordings of Latino music, and everyone seemed to have a fine time. They left in time to prepare for their Christmas Eve midnight worship service.

At about 11:30 PM, one of the older volunteers asked Ed, Gerda, and me to walk with him, as we had all been invited to attend the church service in the village. It promised to be a perfect antidote to the venomous treatment that Josefina had meted out. We walked and stumbled along in the dark over forest paths, and soon came to logs stretched over ravines. Our flashlights seemed to emit only a pinpoint of light. We carefully balanced on the logs, and slid now and then in muddy areas on the path.

We suddenly emerged into a clearing on the edge of a small garden plot and saw a tiny, thatch-roofed, bark-sided church. It was completely dark (no electricity, of course), as were all of the village houses surrounding it. We watched as a number of people who had been inside the church came out and formed a line outside the closed door. We joined them. Each man in the line was given a candle, which they lit one from the other. The leader then knocked on the door and opened it. All of us solemnly filed in and knelt. This was a replica of the little village church in the mountains. At that moment, I missed that little mountain village so much.

We took seats on the roughhewn wooden planks, and by the light of the candles we could see a tree, pine boughs, and a little living manger scene in which a mother and father from the village sat, holding their peacefully sleeping infant. The service was in Q'eqchi, and was led by catechists trained by the diocese. It was beautiful – so simple, so brief, so moving. My eyes filled with tears. At the end, each person knelt before the manger scene and then we all quietly filed out.

We were invited for tamales. The young male volunteer stayed, but Gerda and I declined and started back. As we crossed a field, we heard someone call out to us. Gerda called back. It was the doctor from Wales. She had been called to help a woman named Maria, whose husband was one of the employees at the Refugio. Maria was in labor with their third child. She and her husband were concerned because her second had been an especially difficult labor, and that child is developmentally delayed. We stopped and sat with them for a while in the small thatch-roofed hut. Maria's sleeping platform was separated from the other sleeping mats by a plastic sheet hanging from the ceiling. Her husband lay on the other sleeping platform with their two children. He would help when the baby arrived. After a time, her contractions subsided and we went on back, leaving the doctor to spend the night with the family.

When we reached the center, the generator was off. I was too exhausted to worry about bats and cockroaches. I secured my boots, crawled under my mosquito net and blanket, and slept soundly.

The next day, Christmas morning, Josefina was in a most affable mood. She invited me to help her wrap the gifts that Ed had brought back from the city. They were an embarrassment. Examples were used stuffed animals; cheap, tiny, one-piece plastic dolls; and two piñatas filled with candy. I cheerfully worked with her in wrapping the gifts, and I hoped that the time would pass quickly.

Josefina had set most of the young adult volunteers to work digging for the installation of a septic tank for the pigs. This was poor timing, as she had forgotten that school was out for vacation and there were no planned activities for the children. She worked with some of the cleaning women to get every child scrubbed and dressed in a donated outfit. She asked me to take an individual photo of each child and a group photo for a sort of publicity photo collection.

Gerda had baked four delicious cakes. She happily took time from kitchen duties to help me take the photos of the children. Without mentioning it, I made sure that Zahra was photographed by her and that I was not in the area where her group was gathered.

The gifts and the piñata were well received. Doctor Elin stopped by to say that Maria had still not had her baby and that her husband was drunk and kept shouting for another beer. Celebrations were happening all around us. Fireworks boomed and banged constantly. It was a festive time.

Chapter 8
December 1995
Ordinary Miracles

On the morning of the twenty-sixth, Gerda and I walked past Maria's house. Her husband motioned us in. Maria was lying on her bed, exactly where we had seen her on Christmas Eve. But this time, a tiny, perfectly formed baby girl lay beside her, wrapped in a piece of coarse cotton.

Gerda asked the baby's name, but we were told it was too early for naming. In this low-lying village, there was cholera in the river, and the infant mortality rate was high. Naming is postponed for an extended period of time. I sensed that my Spirit Guides were there, and I imagined them sitting with the Spirits of the baby's ancestors, cross-legged in a circle, grinning like proud grandparents. I had a feeling and a great hope that this baby would survive and thrive!

The ship was due to dock at 2:00. Gerda and I spent the morning visiting some of the homes in the village. Groups of village children joined us, urging us to stop at every home. The village was buzzing with excitement. Everyone was changing to their best clothes and asking to have a photo taken. I was glad to oblige. I planned to give the rolls of film and the money for developing them to whoever was asked to take me to the Airport. Someone here had been designated as my contact, but I had no idea who that would be. I would know soon.

Everyone in the little village was eager to have us visit their home. We sat and talked and laughed with each family. The fathers who had been out gathering wood returned and changed clothes for the photos. The mothers left the cooking fires, but only after serving us their strong coffee-like beverage, laced with much sugar. They dressed themselves and their children in their best outfits and eagerly posed for the camera.

The villagers in these low-lying areas experience great sadness in their lives, including much illness, death, and abuse by employers. One mother recently had her young teenaged son taken by the army to fight in Coban. She worried about him. Some families resist sending their girls to school, even though the teachers are Guatemalan. They want the girls to stay at home and learn the ways of their people and perform the tasks that generations of women have performed: doing laundry at the stream, cooking at the hearth, having and caring for babies. They fear that school may give them ideas about running off to the City and forgetting their families and their traditions.

When we stopped, by invitation, at one house, I recognized the catechist who had led the Christmas Eve service. He and his wife had one of the largest families in the village. Ten children and four adults lived together as members of the extended family. The pictures of Jesus and Mary that had hung in the church were on the wall of the large room in which we sat on benches. A chicken sat on a nest of eggs under one bench beside us.

We sat for a while, and then Gerda asked about the Christmas Eve service. A lively discussion followed in which it was explained that the service was a reenactment of the Posada, which begins with the church door closed. When the door opens, the people walk in with lighted candles, signifying to them the coming of Jesus as he brings new light into the world, and others welcoming him and his message. The people carrying the candles represent those who will carry the light within themselves to others. In the Posada, the parents of Jesus seek a safe place in Bethlehem for shelter as they anticipate his birth. Those who open the door are offering this shelter: a place of refuge in a location far from home.

I asked the catechist and his family what Jesus means to them in their village at the present time in history. He replied, "Jesus is our brother. Like us, he was born poor. He struggled to make people free and to teach them how to live a peaceful life. a peaceful life. He walks with us now as our light, and he asks us to share this light with each other."

Following this beautiful experience, the world shifted a bit and we arrived back at the Refugio at about 1:00. Once there, we began to prepare to go to meet the ship. Josefina came to me to show me a letter and asked me to proofread it. It was addressed to the cruise line whose ship would arrive that day at the dock. It invited and encouraged the cruise company to continue stopping locally and to allow passengers to donate to Casa de La Esperanza while they were docked.

Josefina said that someone had told passengers not to give cash, as it was not safe. (Emily, the former director of volunteers, had told me confidentially that when she was in charge, she had received $1,200 US in cash one day from a ship's passenger, and a total that day of $8,000 US. The problem came when donors specified a use for the money, and then returned at a later time and found no evidence of their requested purchases. In one case, it had been a clothes dryer, and in another, a refrigerator/freezer. Josefina's answer to the complaints was, "We are here to help orphans in the way WE think best. If you want to help the orphans, you will leave the spending of the donations to OUR discretion!").

On this day, Josefina reiterated to me that she is collecting donations to establish a storefront in a nearby town, where she will sell pork and vegetables. She repeated that this would make the orphanage self-sufficient and self-supporting. I listened, and I was again overwhelmed by my powerlessness to "rescue" the children and adults who were caught in this repressive enterprise. My Spirit Guides reminded me that only Love can change the world, and that Love is the light that I can carry within me so that I can attract the possibilities that can transform the world around me.

Meanwhile, there was a vital task to accomplish and a life to salvage. I would have to leave that place soon, but I would never forget or abandon hope for the best life possible for the children, the families, and for Josefina and her husband (who lived in their home country). I hoped that someday Josefina would discover her own inner light and the light of those around her and turn toward it.

Once the letter had been proofread and printed, we set off for the dock. I was not able to say "Goodbye," but I prepared to leave. I packed and shouldered my backpack. The suitcase stayed behind.

Chapter 9
December 1995
Reunion

There was much excitement. The ship had docked! The harbor was bustling with activity. Surrounding the docked ship were a variety of local crafts being sold by merchants arriving in everything from canoes to motorboats. They spread out their wares on the shore or walked around proclaiming loudly that their products were the best. There were the vendors who shouted out their offerings, including excursions to exotic native villages with a restaurant stop and a chance to purchase craft items. Josefina had distributed her letter and brochure, was introducing the passengers to some of the "orphans," and was busily receiving cash donations. She offered a tour of the project, and would soon leave the dock to entertain those passengers who would accompany her. She was totally occupied by the passengers, the photogenic children, and the volunteers.

Ed stepped close to me and whispered, "See the canoe on the right, the one with the men holding up the colorful blanket. I'm your contact. I'm going to hand Zahra to them. Get the children and volunteers to pose for a photo at that moment. Start with the other group, the older ones, not her group. Once she's in the canoe, you and I will leave. Nathan (the volunteer who led us to the church on Christmas Eve) knows only that a home has been found for Zahra. We can trust him to cover and downplay her leaving. Josefina won't miss her. She is in her glory! Nathan will let the other volunteers and the children know that Zahra is safe. "

Suddenly, as I took the photo of the group that was facing away from the canoe, I saw that the blanket had been lowered and the canoe had pulled away. It skimmed smoothly and rapidly over the water in the direction of the mountain village. In it, Zahra had been wrapped in the blanket by her cousins, the two young men from the village whom I knew so well – and she was playing the best game of hide-and-seek of her life! I silently wished Zahra a long and happy life, wiped the tears away as they sprang to my eyes, and turned to follow Ed into a motorboat which took us to the other side of the river, where I was met by a car and driven the 200 miles to the city and the airport. The evening flight to Washington, DC took off on schedule, and suddenly, almost abruptly, I was in the US and in a taxi on my way to the homeless shelter, where friends had gathered for our annual Faith and Resistance Retreat commemorating the Feast of the Holy Innocents.

The Retreat is where we gather to give voice to our prayers and our strong beliefs that as humans, we can learn to be light in a world growing darker – and that true peace is not only possible but necessary! I had been absent from it for several years. It was so good to be able to be with this other, essential part of my family, for even a few days!

Remembering to Dance

Barbara H Mullen Reed, EdD

Remembering to Dance

Chapter 10
December 28, 1995
Retreat to Remember the Holy Innocents Past and Present

Journal Entry:

"It is Thursday, December twenty-eighth, the Feast of the Holy Innocents. We slept last night in the meeting room of a large shelter for the homeless in Washington, DC. Those of us who are going to risk arrest at the Pentagon during our prayer vigil today had a small amount of our own blood drawn by one of the nurses in our group and preserved for today's witness. We will mark a cross on the sidewalk of the Pentagon, and inside the entrance, with this symbol of the blood shed by the innocent children across the ages and by all those those in war who are perpetrators, combatants, or victims. The cross symbolizes the possible fate of those who resist, as Jesus did, any injustice or violence permitted anywhere in the world by those in power. In Biblical terms, blood seals the new covenant of universal love, justice, peace, brotherhood and sisterhood. Its use as a means of resistance indicates for us an appeal to "Stop all Bloodshed."

Our simple liturgy takes place at the homeless shelter and includes
Psalm 124:

> Had not the Lord been with us
> When people rose up against us
> Then they would have swallowed us alive
> When their fury was inflamed against us.

> Then would the waters have overwhelmed us,
> The torrent would have swept over us,
> Over us then would have swept the raging waters.
> Broken was the snare and we were freed.
> Our help is in the name of the Lord who
> Made heaven and earth.

Matthew 2:13-18

> When Herod realized that he had been deceived by the Magi
> He became furious.
> He ordered the massacre of all the boys in Bethlehem and
> Its vicinity two years and under
> In accordance with the time he had
> Ascertained from the Magi.
> Then was fulfilled what had been said
> Through Jeremiah the prophet
> A voice was heard in Ramah
> Sobbing and loud lamentation:
> Rachel weeping for her children
> And she would not be consoled
> Since they were no more.

After the liturgy, we climb into the vans and head for the Pentagon.

The five who will risk arrest are let off near there at 7:30. We walk to the employee entrance. I am wearing the skirt and blouse I wore in Guatemala, along with my winter jacket. I look like I may be coming to work as a civilian employee in the giant complex. Two of us go up to the open door, and we each make the sign of the cross with that tiny amount of our blood on the threshold and inside on the tile. We kneel in prayer at the entrance, holding a sign that asks the US government to stop intervening in support of conflicts around the world that result in the deaths of innocent children and other civilians.

The person who is kneeling with me is immediately arrested and hauled roughly away. I am suddenly alone. At first, I feel guilty, as if I have let everyone down. I was prepared to join in the ministry of those who witness in jail and in prison. Then I tell myself to stop! This is not about me. I am part of an entire universe of love, and we are each and all part of a magnificent web of life. My only role in this is to allow the spirit of love to move into and through me. From this simple acceptance, all power flows.

I move outside into the bleak, cold day and kneel along the frozen grass at the sidewalk edge with others of our little group, so that I can hand out our flyers and ask people who are arriving for work to consider what that work entails. The rest of our friends stand in a large ring of solidarity around us.

I see Arnie Miller in the group, available in case any of us needs legal assistance. Others move in toward the entrance and are arrested. They will present a beautiful witness, both in Court and in jail, to the need for universal peace. I am grateful for all that is, and I join our prayer circle. We thank those who have been handcuffed and are being taken away. The designated support group will be there to help them throughout the day in any way they can.

My Spirit Guides along with Annie, April, and Chad are there. They are close to me, giving me encouragement and comfort. I am humbled and grateful for our Pentagon witness, and for friends who never give up in placing their lives on the line to work for an end to war and injustice.

As we stand together in this loving formation with no beginning or endpoint, I think of the past five years and of the city streets, of the magic of the cave, and of my village home in the mountains. I smile to myself as I wonder where home will be for me next, and when its location will be revealed to me.

I have continued to dance with the Spirits of so many, throughout all dimensions of the universe, wherever I have been led. I have continued to experience peace and great love beyond measure. I glide inwardly into the contentment of this moment, and I feel and breathe in thankfulness for so many opportunities to be with friends and for the continual expansion of the family circle. I feel Chad standing beside and a little behind my left shoulder. He hugs me.

We all stand together in solidarity, and then we join hands and close with a prayer for universal love and peace everywhere. We send ourselves out into ourselves out into the gray winter day with the song, "Down by the Riverside."

Chapter 11
December 1995
A Glimpse at a Sanctuary Movement Priest

Father Liam refused to accumulate possessions. He owned only two suits of clothes, each the plain, black, understated garb of a priest. He refused to own a car or a house, condo or cabin. He chose to be unencumbered and to be free to travel wherever he was needed. He remembered well the conversations at the Seminary in Ireland where he had studied, and from where he had been ordained a priest. He, like many others at the time, was from a large, poor family. There was always encouragement for parents to produce many sons and daughters so that some could be given to the Church as nuns and priests. His family had included 11 children, and it was economically impossible for them to subsist without some of the offspring entering religious orders at an early age.

Liam had been determined to do the work to which he believed God called him as a priest. He had loved the Mass and the Church as long as he could remember. When he was about ten years old, a young parish priest had caught his attention as the priest spoke of the biblical mandate of Matthew Chapter 25.

31: "When the Son of Man comes in his glory, and all the angels with him, he will sit on his glorious throne.

32: All the nations will be gathered before him, and he will separate the people one from another as a shepherd separates the sheep from the goats.

33: He will put the sheep on his right and the goats on his left.

34: "Then the King will say to those on his right, 'Come, you who are blessed by my Father; take your inheritance, the kingdom prepared for you since the creation of the world.
35: For I was hungry and you gave me something to eat, I was thirsty and you gave me something to drink, I was a stranger and you invited me in.
36: I needed clothes and you clothed me, I was sick and you looked after me, I was in prison and you came to visit me.'
37: "Then the righteous will answer him, 'Lord, when did we see you hungry and feed you, or thirsty and give you something to drink?
38: When did we see you a stranger and invite you in, or needing clothes and clothe you?
39: When did we see you sick or in prison and go to visit you?'
40: "The King will reply, 'Truly I tell you, whatever you did for one of the least of these brothers and sisters of mine, you did for me.'
41: "Then he will say to those on his left, 'Depart from me, you who are cursed, into the eternal fire prepared for the devil and his angels.
42: For I was hungry and you gave me nothing to eat, I was thirsty and you gave me nothing to drink,
43: I was a stranger and you did not invite me in, I needed clothes and you did not clothe me, I was sick and in prison and you did not look after me.'
44: "They also will answer, 'Lord, when did we see you hungry or thirsty or a stranger or needing clothes or sick or in prison, and did not help you?'
45: "He will reply, 'Truly I tell you, whatever you did not do for one of the least of these, you did not do for me.'
46: "Then they will go away to eternal punishment, but the righteous to eternal life."

Remembering to Dance

Though he held a very different view of Heaven and of Second Chances, Father Liam had never veered at all from the belief that the mandate for a Christian and the privilege of any priestly advisors was to follow the compassionate words of Jesus spoken in Matthew 25 to the letter. He firmly believed that the "threatening language" as to separating sheep from goats and consigning some people to eternal hell fire had been added to the account by an unknown editor long after Jesus had transitioned from his earthly visit to the heavenly realm. Jesus had never hurt, injured, or condemned any person during his time on earth, and it was impossible for Father Liam to believe that Jesus would do so at any future time.

This was his belief and his practice. He had wanted to become a priest in the United States because of the great need he saw for priests who were willing to identify with "the least of these" and to learn to serve them adequately. Others in his seminary classes had spoken of the wealth to be accumulated in the United States, especially in resort areas from parishioners with seemingly unlimited funds. He knew that some had been tempted by the large amounts of cash collected each Sunday and had even convinced themselves that it was all right for a priest to keep all the cash from a "Father's Day" collection at their church, and other cash donations as well. The practice of opening and discarding the envelopes in the collection plate and pocketing the cash to be found therein had become commonplace in some parishes. Further rationalization decreed that priests worked hard and deserved some time to wager at the racetrack or to enjoy complimentary rooms and the thrill of gaming at lavish casinos.

This was not for Father Liam. He was loved by almost everyone, feared by some for his strong and focused beliefs, and usually in trouble for calling the Church hierarchy to account for its indiscretions and inaction.

His identification with those in need had led him to form connections between the USA and Central America. He had learned Spanish and several of the native languages. He had worked to bring victims of the wars in Central America to safe sanctuaries across the border. His networks were extensive, and the schools and work opportunities he envisioned and then created in cooperation with many others were legendary.

Tonight, he would take time off for a few hours and visit a missionary priest friend. Tonight, he and his friend would ask each other the impossible questions that always surfaced: "Why do dedicated Christian believers allow children to live on the streets in places like Guatemala City, where they are the victims of predators who bribe them with lethal drugs so that they will commit crimes? "Why do these same exemplary believers allow kidnapped babies to be sold for adoption to innocent victims?" and so many more! The answers would not be apparent, but the tasks at hand would be clear. The hope was kept alive that the people who want to be followers of the Word will have "eyes to see and ears to hear," and will be willing to come together to do the hard work of making the necessary changes.

This is what they considered worth giving their lives for. This was their calling and their destiny.

Chapter 12
December 1995-January 1996
Sanctuary

The 1970s presented an unexpected challenge to the Catholic Church that continues many years later. Via Vatican Council II, Divine Source had thrown open the windows of that ancient institution and had let in fresh air and a steady stream of light. All over the world, nuns and priests examined their roles, and many began to see themselves in this increased illumination as servants of God called not just to monastic withdrawal and solitude but to actual interaction with people of all ages and life conditions. They began to feel and experience their humanness in a whole new way. True missionary work came to be understood not as forcing others into certain belief patterns, but as ministering to the needs of human beings everywhere as brothers and sisters.

One day, sometime in the 1980s, at our parish in Florida, heard an extraordinary interview on National Public Radio. A cloistered Carmelite nun named Sister Lucy Poulin had, with others, formed a cooperative community called H.O.M.E., Inc. in the early 1970's. This action had caused her to be dismissed from her religious Order, as she was deemed to have a lack of understanding of the life of contemplative prayer. The ouster did not deter her from her path as a holy person and as a deeply spiritual "doer of the Word."

She had brought together in a remote village in rural Maine a group of women who had lost their only means of employment when the one local industry, a shoe factory, had closed. The idea was to have them engage in home industries such as sewing that would provide goods that could be sold to support them and their families. One thing led to another, and soon the need for reading instruction became apparent. A school program was started, along with other offshoots, to meet nutritional needs, childcare, housing, and gardening.

In the next decade, amid violence in Central American countries such as El Salvador and Guatemala, families fleeing for their lives and seeking shelter in the USA also arrived, and were given sanctuary there. Strangers in a strange land, they were not just given shelter, but they also became part of the unique program that had evolved from Sr. Lucy's ministrations. In the radio interview, she explained that she had thought initially that she would find a way to help the refugee women retain their weaving skills in their new home country. She soon discovered that although they quickly picked up a few words of spoken English, the women were unable to read in any language.

She had hoped to make them self-sustaining, and had arranged for donations of sewing machines and patterns so that they could make and sell clothing in addition to the weaving. The fact that they could not read, though they were skillful at sewing, was holding them back. This required the introduction of classes in reading, writing, and other useful subjects. The need for housing became apparent as more families from both the US and Central America arrived. This led to a program of instruction in building houses for the men and women who were interested in learning these skills.

Cooking classes followed. Weaving and embroidery were popular pursuits. Medicinal plants and home remedies were integrated with the community's knowledge of Western medicine. Growing vegetables became a popular activity. Classes in childbirth and childcare were added. Eventually there was also hospitality offered to local homeless persons and a meal program. AA meetings were added to the course list, and a little church was built for worship services. A number of former college students traveling the country during the restless, impassioned era following the Vietnam War became some of the early, dedicated volunteers.

It was to this amazing community that Arnie Miller arranged transport for Gabor, Colel, and little Xena. The harsh Maine climate in winter would be a challenge, but they were young and strong and would thrive there, he was sure. There was also the advantage that, if pursued for any reason, they could slip over the border into Canada and be safe.

The system that was in place to provide safe passage for refugees fleeing for their lives was the twentieth-century version of the Underground Railway. Many of the persons linked across the continents in this life-saving enterprise were brought together through their church affiliations. A large number of them were Roman Catholics. Lay persons, priests, and nuns created and sustained many of the smoothly functioning networks. I knew of the Sanctuary movement through contacts over the years in parishes in the southwestern United States, across the country, and from Florida to the Canadian border.

Colel, Gabor, and Xena had traveled from Guatemala City to the United States by automobile, starting early in the evening of the day that I had left them at the lawyer's office. This was a dangerous undertaking. The syndicate members responsible for the kidnaping of Xena had lost out on the collection of their anticipated fee for her adoption. They would be attempting to trace her immediate whereabouts in the hope of retrieving their lost commodity. An attempt by them to abort any border crossing would not be out of the question. The arrangements had been made to pay the driver, and to provide the necessary bribes at the borders of Guatemala and Mexico, and later between Mexico and the United States. The last leg of the journey from Guatemala City to the Mexican border was in a truck. The baby was mercifully quiet and content in her new infant car seat, and the truck rumbled smoothly through the checkpoint as the envelope was passed from the driver to the border guard at the checkpoint on each side. Colel, Xena, and Gabor now had Guatemalan birth certificates that were priceless commodities, but as yet they had no visas that would allow legal entry into the United States. The truck took them as far as Tucson, where they spent the night with friends of the Sanctuary movement, who fed them and gave them warm clothing and blankets.

In the morning, they met the Catholic priest who would drive them to the Washington, DC area. Father Joe was a rugged outdoorsman who was at least six feet tall and had tousled, ginger-colored hair, kind green eyes, and a reddish-brown beard. He often walked the border between Mexico and the US and had saved many lives by providing food and water to travelers seeking asylum. He could speak Spanish, of which they understood little. Their village in Guatemala was one of the few that had rebelled at learning the "language of the conquerors" and had ruled out using Spanish names for their children. There was no village school, so, except for the village catechists, there was little opportunity to converse with outsiders or to learn other languages.

Somehow, though, they had no trouble communicating with this brave man. He found music on the car radio that they all liked, and the miles went by rapidly. They took a few rest stops, but Father Joe insisted that they keep going and that he was at his best when he was at the wheel on a long drive. The weather was chilly, but not really cold, until they reached Virginia. There, the mountains, the valleys, the trees, the roads were all covered in snow! They all took a break and got out to experience the wonder of the cold whiteness. Back in the car, with the heater working smoothly, Colel and Xena fell asleep.

When they awoke, the car had stopped at a building which Father Joe told them was "Casa de Sanctuary," though they had no idea what he had said. They would all stay there for two days, then start out again for their new home. They were greeted at once and invited into a small hallway that led to a most welcome sight... a line of little bedrooms, each with its own small sink and running water! All around them were voices speaking in the strange (and often loud) language of the gringos. They took their blankets, washed, and gratefully lay down on the double bed. As Xena contentedly nursed, Gabor and Colel talked softly together and did what they could to make sense of all that was happening to them.

They knew that the Spirits of their ancestors could be anywhere, and were surely accompanying them now. They were protected in a way that they had understood from childhood, and they would trust in these Spirits and in God to guide them along the safest path. They all slept as the clamor of voices surrounded them in the hallway, and doors opened and closed.

As soon as they had finished dressing the next morning, a soft knock on the door startled them. A woman who identified herself as Sister Margaret stood in the hallway. She smiled and opened her arms to them in a gesture of welcome. Colel could not hold back her tears at this loving gesture and began to cry and smile at the same time. Sr. Margaret put her arms around Colel and spoke softly to her in Spanish until the tears subsided. Then she went over to Xena, and looking back at Colel and gesturing, asked if she could hold the baby. Xena sensed that she was in the presence of a friend, and smiled and cooed. Sr. Margaret sat down on the bed and gently rocked the baby while Colel straightened the room and neatly piled up their new winter clothing.

Sr. Margaret handed the baby to Colel and motioned to them to follow her. They entered the dining room, in which about thirty people sat at long tables, companionably drinking coffee and eating a simple breakfast. Soon, to their delight, Colel and Gabor were seated in front of a plate of tortillas and eggs. This was a spectacular meal, they decided. When the last bite was gone, and the coffee cups were empty, Sr. Margaret returned and explained with gestures that it was time for school.

Chapter 13
January 1996
Lessons

This was a totally unexpected development for Gabor and Colel! They had known that they would be spending the day in what was called Maryland (unpronounceable to them) before going on to the place known as Maine, (also unpronounceable), but they had certainly not considered that they would be in SCHOOL! It was okay, though. There were positive advantages to this strange gringo land. One benefit was definitely the indoor toilets and sinks with immediate hot and cold water. After some interaction with these marvelous amenities, they were directed to what was labeled "Classroom." They sat at one of the many tables, with another couple who also held an infant strapped to the mother in a colorful blanket. The teacher was a woman who was dressed in jeans and a sweater and had long brown hair that she wore in a braid that extended for some distance down her back. She stood at the front of the room.

The teacher motioned to a man to come to the front of the room for a demonstration.

"Good Morning!" she said to him and shook his hand. "My name is Maggie."

"Good Morning, Maggie", the man replied. "My name is Juan."

Several volunteers went to the front to repeat and practice this exercise using their own names. They wore necklaces made of elastic cord and stiff paper around their necks. Squares of the stiff paper were passed out to everyone, and the students wrote on them with a pen (often with difficulty.) Colel and Gabor did not know what to do. Maggie appeared with papers, said something to them and gestured that they were to copy what she had written on a paper. Maggie gestured to Xena also, but they did not know why.

All in all, it was quite an ordeal, and they were glad when school was over at the end of the hour. The rest of the morning passed quickly, as they were directed to join others in the clothing area to sort donated clothing into sizes. There was a huge pile that did not seem to diminish no matter how rapidly they worked. Within about three hours it was sorted into individual bins and ready for distribution.

Colel missed the interaction among the women that would have occurred in their home village. The women might have spent time together milling corn or weaving, and occasionally chatting softly as they worked. These women in Maryland talked a lot, in a language that was totally unintelligible to her. The voices seemed loud and harsh, but the women smiled and appeared to welcome her. Still, a feeling of utter loneliness brought tears to her eyes from time to time.

Gabor had gone outside wearing his new warm winter jacket and gloves to work with the other men, shoveling snow from the sidewalks and paths. He felt lonely too, and he wondered what useful work he could do in this vast country that observed so many strange and complicated customs.

A light lunch was served, parents took children to their rooms for their afternoon naps, and it was quiet for about an hour. Around 2:00, Father Joe suddenly knocked on their door. When they opened it, he motioned to Colel and Gabor and Xena to join him. The parents sat down in chairs around a table in his office, holding little Xena close. They were soon joined by a short man with a ruddy face, black hair, and twinkling eyes that seemed to be green at one moment and blue the next. He was introduced as Father Liam O'Reilly. The first words uttered by Father Liam were a miracle to Colel and Gabor. They were in Q'eqchi.

Chapter 14
January 2, 1996
Hope

Like parched earth responding to a gentle, steady rain, Colel and Gabor absorbed and drank thirstily from the words of this most unlikely of messengers, who was surely an angel. Tears sprang to their eyes once again. Father Liam looked directly at them with his dancing blue-green eyes, and smiled. Then they all laughed and began a conversation that went so rapidly that Father Joe had difficulty interrupting to say pleasantly that he would see them later as he left the room to attend to his duties in the house.

At last, the couple could tell the story of the kidnapping at the market; their puzzling and miraculous reunion with their daughter; their meeting in the lawyer's office; their sudden departure from Guatemala, first in a car and then in a truck; and their crossing of the Mexican border and entry into the USA. Then there was the long drive with their new friend, Father Joe, and their welcome at the Casa. It was way beyond overwhelming for people who had never ventured far from their mountain village, and had always done so by walking.

Father Liam listened in a way that was reassuring and comforting and helped them to accept that all of this had actually happened. They were safe. No one would be looking for them. Father Liam gently placed his hand on each of their heads in turn, and said a prayer of blessing for Colel, for Gabor, and for Xena. After this, the young parents dried their tears and smiled gratefully at the priest.

Father Liam spent about an hour with them after that, explaining carefully where they were going and what to expect. He told them that at least one family at the community in

Maine spoke and understood their language, so they would not be alone in that way again. He patiently answered each of their questions.

He spread out a map of Central America and of the United States and helped them trace the route of the part of their journey that was complete and the part that would start the next day.

He also assured them that they would quickly learn English, and that this would be best under the circumstances. He agreed that it would be difficult, but that, like Mary and Joseph in the nativity story, they were doing this to protect the life of their child, and he believed that the opportunity to flee to safety was a gift from God and from the Spirits that guide each of us wherever we are.

Father Liam would drive them to Maine, starting early the next morning, January 3rd, as soon as it was daylight. Colel and Gabor listened, but it was beyond their capacity to understand, as so much had happened to them in such a short time. They spoke quietly to each other. They were part of a miracle. They would trust. Wonderful smells of food cooking were beginning to fill the hall as they went out and walked with Father Liam toward the dining room.

They sat at a table with a group of people from El Salvador. Father Liam entertained with jokes and stories in Spanish, English, and some occasional translations, for their benefit, in Q'eqchi. It was clear that he was loved by all, and that he was a source of boundless energy and caring. There were many comments on Xena's beauty. She smiled in the midst of the din of all the voices, and her parents tried to relax.

After dinner, there was a short prayer service, and then some guitar players brought out their instruments and everyone sang folk songs in English and in Spanish. Music is its own universal language, and Colel and Gabor went to bed extremely happy and excited about what was to happen in their lives.

Before daylight the next morning, Sister Margaret served them breakfast and tucked them safely into the sturdy Ford Taurus for the journey to their new home in the snowy state of Maine. The seating arrangement was the same as it had been with Father Joe. Colel sat buckled in the back seat, and Gabor and Father Liam in the front. Little Xena was next to her mother, lying in her infant car seat. She raised no objection, as her mother's hand gently caressed her and the rhythm of the moving car lulled her to sleep.

The roads were clear, the day promised to be sunny, and the little family exchanged hugs with Sister Margaret. Colel and Gabor felt a mixture of excitement for what was to come and an unexpected sadness to be saying goodbye to this compassionate woman, whom they had known for only a day or two, but who seemed to be a permanent part of their family.

Father Liam proved to be a good driver (though a speedy one) and a wonderful travelling companion. As they drove through places whose names they could not begin to comprehend or remember – Maryland, New Jersey, New York, Connecticut, Massachusetts, New Hampshire, and Maine. He had interesting stories to tell about each place. It was dark when they turned at a battered sign that marked the road to a cooperative community in Orland, Maine.

The snow-covered scene that greeted them as they turned down the lane to the community was totally unexpected. The place was illuminated by the moon, and many stars, in a clear night sky. There were simple wood-frame buildings everywhere. There was a little church, a barn, and a number of houses, mostly under construction, strewn about the property. They could see such beauty in the simplicity of this sparkling snow scene. Their first impression was that this was a place of welcome. One knock on the door, and it burst open to the chorus of joyful hospitality. It was a place of people working to build something that could be of use to many who shared a dream of coming together to find hope and a peaceful life.

There were men, women, and a few older children who were still not asleep for the night, ready to greet them as they stood hesitantly just inside the doorway leading to the warm kitchen. They received Father Liam enthusiastically, with big hugs, pats on the back, and offers of food and coffee. He put his arms around the shoulders of Colel and Gabor, who were standing off to the side, shyly off to the side, and told everyone first in English, then in Spanish, and finally in Q'eqchi, that this new family was looking forward to becoming a part of the community. As always, details of their situation were not necessary and were not revealed. There was always a chance that someone on the property might be there to gather such information.

Father Liam had made sure that the couple who spoke Q'eqchi would be there to welcome the travelers. He introduced Colel and Gabor to Cadmael and his wife Akna. Cadmael looked like a younger version of Eadrich, with the same laughing eyes and tall, slender frame. Gabor and he liked each other at once. Akna was short in stature, with sparkling, dark eyes and a round, gentle face. She was somewhat shy. At first, she stood a little behind her husband, but her broad smile soon burst forth as she heard the men conversing in the familiar sounds of her native language, and she felt the connection to the village life that they both missed so much. Akna explained that their children were asleep, but that they would all be together at breakfast in the morning. All four of them embraced and then went off into a corner, where they began a rapid and extensive conversation.

Colel and Gabor were grateful to have the opportunity to share their impressions of this confusing land with someone who came from common roots. They expressed their disbelief at the size of the rooms, the furnishings, the kitchens, the vast amounts of food, at so many things that boggled the mind. They all laughed, they cried, and they bonded as friends for life.

Everyone else drank coffee and ate cake and carried on a lively political discussion with Father Liam until their guest of honor decided that he had to be on his way. He would stay nearby that night, and the next day, with a Maryknoll missionary priest friend. The two would be consuming much whiskey as they brought each other up to date on their work. They would recount tall tales, jokes, and stories from their native Ireland, and would reexamine their shared view of theology and recommit to their belief in working for a just and loving society.

Chapter 15
January 1996
The Feast of the Three Kings
Melchior, Gaspar, and Balthazar

Matthew Chapter 2:

1: "After Jesus had been born at Bethlehem in Judaea during the reign of King Herod, suddenly some wise men came to Jerusalem from the east,
2: asking, 'Where is the infant king of the Jews? We saw his star as it rose and have come to do him homage.'
3: When King Herod heard this he was perturbed, and so was the whole of Jerusalem.
4: He called together all the chief priests and the scribes of the people, and enquired of them where the Christ was to be born.
5: They told him, 'At Bethlehem in Judaea, for this is what the prophet wrote:
6: And you, Bethlehem, in the land of Judah, you are by no means the least among the leaders of Judah, for from you will come a leader who will shepherd my people Israel.'
7: Then Herod summoned the wise men to see him privately. He asked them the exact date on which the star had appeared
8: and sent them on to Bethlehem with the words, 'Go and find out all about the child, and when you have found him, let me know, so that I too may go and do him homage.'
9: Having listened to what the king had to say, they set out. And suddenly the star they had seen rising went forward and halted over the place where the child was.

10: The sight of the star filled them with delight, and going into the house they saw the child with his mother Mary, and falling to their knees they did him homage. Then, opening their treasures, they offered him gifts of gold and frankincense and myrrh.
12: But they were given a warning in a dream not to go back to Herod, and returned to their own country by a different way.
13: After they had left, suddenly the angel of the Lord appeared to Joseph in a dream and said, 'Get up, take the child and his mother with you, and escape into Egypt, and stay there until I tell you, because Herod intends to search for the child and do away with him.'
14: So Joseph got up and, taking the child and his mother with him, left that night for Egypt,
15: where he stayed until Herod was dead."

The holiday that is observed in Guatemala and other parts of Central America as the celebration of the giving of gifts in honor of the arrival of Jesus, is the Feast of the Three Kings, El Dia de Reyes which is celebrated on January sixth. To Guatemalans, this is the traditional day of giving and receiving gifts in honor of the birth of Jesus, whom many believe to be the incarnation of God in this world.

Like Colel, Gabor, and Xena, the holy family in the Biblical account fled from danger in their home country and settled in a strange land, far away from their family and their native culture, language, and customs.

How is such a feast day celebrated in a place of sanctuary for the uprooted wanderers in our modern society?

At their place of refuge, the holiday started as did every day with a brief gathering to remember all who were struggling in the world for any reason. Colel and Gabor and Xena were greeted by their friends Akna and Cadmael, and their two little boys, aged two and three. The boys resembled their mother in stature and appearance, but definitely had their father's outgoing personality. They immediately asked if Gabor could come to the barn with them to change the straw for the calves. Cadmael smiled indulgently and told them that he would check the chart to see to what chores the newcomers had been assigned. As it turned out, Colel and Gabor had been assigned to work with Cadmael and Akna's family. Cadmael explained this to the delight of his little son.

Immediately after that, by about 5:30 AM, the farm chores began. Colel and Gabor, with Xena comfortably secured to her mother's back, shyly joined the others and were immediately swept into the organized chaos that accompanied the feeding of chickens, cows, and goats. They cleaned the barn stalls and put down fresh bedding, and also fed and bedded the calves. They did the milking by hand. Then there were eggs o gather. Everyone worked together everyone worked together in a way that reminded the newcomers of the rhythm of life in their faraway village in the mountains. Children and grownups all participated.

Returning to the communal kitchen after chores, they found that the Three Kings had left a little gift for each of the children. They were beautifully handcrafted objects. There were little dolls, some intricately carved objects such as animals and birds, little replicas of furniture, and small woven coverlets for the tiny beds. Gabor turned the little bird over in his hand that had been given to them for Xena. They would treasure it and keep it for her until she was a little older. It reminded him of the intricate carvings he had been taught to do by his father and grandfather through the years. Yes, this little bird embodied the Spirits of those who had formed it, and the

Spirits of the forest from which the wood had been gathered. He was going to be at home here.

Breakfast brought more bustling and structured confusion. After an amazing meal featuring fresh milk and eggs and home-baked bread, many again ventured out into the biting cold to start on the next round of chores. There were about fifty people in all, including the children. They divided themselves into groups of about ten each, and rotated occasionally from one job to another, so that everyone was able to help wherever needed.

Gabor was asked to join the crew of men and women, which included Akna and Cadmael, that was insulating some of the houses that were under construction. The little boys would go to their classrooms for two hours of school, followed by a short period of supervised outdoor play in the snow before lunch. Colel and Xena would go to the part of the building that was used for classrooms and would do some weaving with a group of eight others. Colel was thrilled, and once again found tears of gratitude welling up in her eyes as they walked into the room that was simple in style, but well equipped with looms and all of the necessary equipment for spinning, weaving and sewing.

Sister Ellen, one of the teachers, had joined them. She began to explain to Colel about the classes. The purpose was to provide instruction for guests, and also for women in the neighboring towns and villages who were unemployed. A thriving home-based business was developing, while the endangered arts of sewing, spinning, and weaving were being salvaged. Love and respect for the earth, for each other, and for the gifts of creation: that was the credo of the place that had become their home.

All of this was translated for Colel by one of the staff who was from El Salvador, but who also spoke and understood the

Q'eqchi language. Colel nodded and smiled, but she was still overwhelmed by the whirlwind of events that had occurred in such a short time. When the demonstration was over and the others had left, and as she and Xena sat quietly in a corner of the room and gradually relaxed, she felt a tingling sensation throughout her body and the familiar strong connection with the Spirits of the Ancestors. She felt the tenderness and encouragement of the Creator Mother, and she let herself slide quietly into this familiar and comforting reservoir of strength that both nurtured and empowered.

As she nursed Xena, she was comforted by the gradual and illuminating revelation that it would be best to focus on one thing each day, rather than to try to comprehend all of it at once. Today, she would learn the system of weaving that these calm and capable men and women used. She would find in the thread and the colors and their interconnectedness the familiar path to her heart. She would continue, as always, on that welcoming path to the divine source of all love and light and, with every step and every breath, she would feel thankfulness for all that is.

THE END

Afterword

It was not until more than a year later, in the spring of 1997, that I visited Arnie and Chris Miller at their home in Maryland, and heard the details of the journey of Colel, Gabor, and little Xena from Guatemala to Maine.

Their adjustment to life in Maine, Arnie reported, had been smooth. He also had recently heard that Gabor was happily employed in the sawmill on premises. He and Colel were expecting a new baby in a few months. Colel was taking classes in speaking and reading English. She continued with her favorite crafts of spinning and weaving. The baby, Xena, was cheerfully walking, and beginning to talk in sentences. Xena imitated the other children, so the majority of her speech was in English. They showed me a group picture that had been sent by Sister Linda, with everyone gathered in the kitchen of the community center celebrating the Feast of the Three Kings that past January. There were happy smiles and joy all around. I have frequently thought of that picture. It keeps me smiling with gratitude for friends and for community.

My life, recently, has focused on local parish work with adults and children, and with our outreach mostly to veterans who have returned from Iraq and elsewhere with PTSD and related medical conditions, which have caused many of them to be without family support and without a place to call home.

It is my hope and my dream to return one day to Guatemala and to see in person my friends in the village. I am told that there is a wonderful new school and medical facility being built along the river. It is dedicated to empowering local indigenous people in combining their knowledge of native medicinal remedies with some of the beneficial practices of Western medicine. There will be classes taught in Q'eqchi for both girls and boys. The staff and directors of the project will be almost exclusively local residents. A school boat will transport students to the school from their villages along and above the river. The students will be trained for local jobs, and new jobs will be created for them.

It is a new day, and hope is high. I want so much to continue to be a part of it.

Notes

I. The Sanctuary Movement

The Central American Resource Center (CARECEN), originally named the Central American Refugee Center, was established in 1981 and incorporated in 1982 to meet the needs of refugees fleeing a period of violence and strife in Central America. El Salvador, Nicaragua and Guatemala all experienced civil wars during the 1980s and 1990s, and Honduras suffered more than a decade of civil strife in the form of a "dirty war." Many Central Americans, seeking refuge from the violence in their home countries, fled to neighboring nations, including Mexico and the United States.

The founders of CARECEN recognized the need for an organization to protect the rights of Central American refugees, seeking shelter in Washington, D.C., from conflict in their home countries. While CARECEN was first established as a direct legal service agency, over the past three decades the organization has evolved and adapted to the current needs of Washington's Latino community. Today our programs provide direct services in immigration, housing, and citizenship, while also promoting empowerment, civil-rights advocacy, and civic training for Latinos.

What follows is a timeline of some of the most significant moments in CARECEN's history.

CARECEN established itself as a safe haven for Central American refugees and a hub of community education and organizing to advocate for the protection of human and civil rights. CARECEN mobilized support for the granting of refugee status to Central Americans already in the United

States, and began training "rights promoters" to educate the community on worker, immigrant, and tenant rights.

In 1985, CARECEN played a formative role in the initial stages of Casa de Maryland, which provided emergency clothing, food, immigration assistance, and English instruction to new immigrants. In this year, the American Baptist Church (ABC) won a key suit against the Immigration and Naturalization Service (INS): American Baptist Church v. Thornburgh. CARECEN responded to this modest victory with an organizing and coalition development drive to advocate for suspension of deportation, and permanent residency, for eligible Guatemalans and Salvadorans in the "ABC class."

II. Amnesty International Report May 1992

"GUATEMALA"

Children in fear Street children and street educators continue to be targeted

INTRODUCTION

According to charitable agencies working with street children in Guatemala, there are some 5,000 street children living on the streets of Guatemala City. Over the last two years Amnesty International has been deeply disturbed at reports of human rights abuses, including, beatings, torture, "disappearances" and extrajudicial executions, reportedly carried out against street children by official security force agents, particularly the police, acting sometimes in plain clothes and sometimes in uniform. In other cases, abuses have been carried out by agents of private security firms which operate under license from the National Police and the Ministry of the Interior. (See Guatemala: Extrajudicial Executions and Human Rights Violations against Street Children, AMR 34/37/90 of August 1990, which documented many of these cases and Guatemala: Criminal Proceedings: Human Rights Violations against Street Children, AI Index: AMR 34/20/91 of May 1991).

Abuses against street children continue to take place in the context of police claims of a spiraling crime rate, particularly in the capital, Guatemala City. A special task force called Hunapú (Hunters), comprising members of the Policía Nacional (PN), National Police, the Policía de Hacienda (Treasury Police) and the Policía Militar Ambulante (PMA), Mobile Military Police, came into force in February 1992 to combat common crime in Guatemala, replacing the integrated services police unit

Barbara H Mullen Reed, EdD

Sistema de Protección Cívica (SIPROCI), System of Civil Protection. The police maintain that, in Guatemala City, gangs of street youths (called maras) are responsible for high levels of crime. Abuses against petty criminals and street children are not a new phenomenon, but cases have been coming to light over the past two years because an agency working with such children has begun pressing for inquiries into the abuses. In some cases, testimonies given by the children have then led to new abuses against them, as the police apparently are trying to intimidate, and even eliminate, those who have incriminated the police in crimes such as the beating, "disappearance", and extrajudicial execution of street children.

Street educators and those working with street children have also been targeted by the security forces, either because of their work protecting street children from abuse, because they have denounced human rights violations against street children or because they have provided evidence as witnesses in judicial proceedings against members of the security forces charged with human rights violations against street children. Amnesty International also believes that street educators and those working with street children have been targeted in an effort to intimidate the workers of Covenant House (Casa Alianza), an organization which helps street children in Guatemala, in bringing the perpetrators of human rights violations to justice. In two incidents, both July 1991, unidentified gunmen opened fire on Covenant House's Crisis Centre and on Covenant House's Legal Office in Guatemala City. Nobody was hurt in either incident. In one incident, one of the assailants shouted "Vamos a ametrallar a Bruce Harris y tomar fotos de todo el personal para matarlos a ellos y a los niños" ("we are going to shoot Bruce Harris[1] and take photographs of all the staff and

---

[1] Bruce Harris was the Executive Director of Covenant House for Latin America

we are going to shoot them and the children"). Covenant House attributed these attacks to the opening of the Legal Office of Covenant House, which has been in the forefront of efforts to push for investigations into police abuses against street children.

Furthermore, Amnesty International is concerned that the impunity with which the police appear to operate against street children in Guatemala may be encouraging indiscriminate attacks against them by civilians in Guatemala City. In the past year the number of attacks on street children by men in civilian clothes has increased. In a recent incident reported to Amnesty International two street children were severely beaten by two market sellers in the Barajuste market in Guatemala City on 20 March 1992. The sellers who, reportedly, blamed the street children for a drop in sales in the market, beat one of the children with a metal tube on the chest, arms and legs and beat the other on the right leg and left arm. The children later reported that one of the sellers shouted "si la policía no los ha matado, nosotros lo vamos a hacer" ("if the police haven't killed you already we will do it ourselves").

Despite legal proceedings against members of the police or private police, only in isolated cases have investigations resulted in the prosecution of those responsible.

Incidents of human rights violations

I Street children

1. José Vidal, 17 Nelson Larios, 13 Juan López González (alias "Tijuana"), 13 Mario René Hernández Aguirre (alias "El Muerto"), 17 Fernando Sarceño, 17 Axel Belmin Tenas, 17 Ana María Quiej (female), 15 Melvin Enrique Girón, 14 Omar Francisco Morán, 14

These nine street children were arrested and beaten by members of the recently formed combined security force unit Hunapú in Guatemala City on different occasions in March 1992.

On 19 March, at approximately 10:00am, in the Barajuste market in Zone 1 of Guatemala City, street children José Vidal, Nelson Larios, José López González and Mario René Hernández Aguirre were reportedly detained by four members of Hunapú. The children were forcibly shoved into a police car belonging to the transport department of the National Police and driven away. According to the children's account, they were beaten inside the vehicle and then thrown out of it in Zone 3 of the city, while it was still in motion. José López González was previously detained and beaten on 6 March 1992 by more than 35 members of the PMA, together with more than 15 other street children and youths (see case of Moisés Rivas et al, described below).

On the same day at approximately 2:30pm, in Zone 1 of Guatemala City, street children Fernando Sarceño and Axel Belmin Tenas were reportedly detained by two members of Hunapú. The incident again occurred in Zone 1 of Guatemala City, in front of a children's shelter run by Covenant House. The agents, one a member of the National Police and the other a member of the PMA, made the children stand up against a wall and searched them. According to a witness, who also noted the identification number of one of the policemen, the PMA agent hit Fernando Sarceño in the stomach. The two children were subsequently released.

Also on the same day, at approximately 5:00pm, in front of the shelter of Covenant House, two members of Hunapú, one belonging to the National Police and the other to the PMA, reportedly detained Mario René Hernández Aguirre (who had been detained earlier the same day) and Ana María Quiej. The

PMA agent searched the children and subsequently started beating Mario René Hernández with the butt of his rifle. A security guard at the Covenant House refuge witnessed the incident and tried to intervene, telling the policemen to stop beating the children. The policemen subsequently left. The security guard noted the identification number of one of the policemen, who it was later revealed was the same policeman allegedly involved in the beating of Fernando Sarceño and Axel Belmin Tenas.

On the previous day, 18 March, at approximately 5:00pm in the Barajuste market, street children Melvin Enrique Girón and Omar Francisco Morán were reportedly detained by two members of Hunapú, one of whom was a member of the National Police and one of whom was a member of the PMA. The boys claim the PMA agent hit them on the head and back and gave Melvin Enrique Girón electric shocks with a bastón chino (a type of truncheon with an electric prod at its tip), before taking them to the San José Pinula detention centre.

2. Moisés Rivas, 15 Marvin Antonio Mejía (alias Diego Chouza Franco), 16 Manuel López, 16 Carlos Antonio Contreras, 17 Boris Velásquez, about 17 Juan López González, "Tijuana", about 12 Erick Mendoza López, "Lepra", about 17 José R. López

According to reports received by Amnesty International, at about 1.30 pm on 6 March 1992, about 35 agents of the PMA cordoned off four blocks of Zone 1 of Guatemala City and violently arrested 16 street children and youths. According to witnesses, some of the children were beaten by the police as they were rounded up. The majority of them were then handcuffed and, when the PMA ran out of handcuffs, ropes were used to tie the children and youths. A staff member of Covenant House who witnessed the incident told the PMA agents that, according to the Código del Menor (Code of Minors) they should not handcuff minors. The PMA agents, however, replied that they were "órdenes de la superioridad" ("orders from higher up").

The minors among the group were taken to the Segundo Cuerpo (Second Precinct) of the National Police, again in apparent contravention of the Code of Minors, which states that when children are detained they must be sent to the Juvenile Court (Magistratura de Menores) or to the Justice of the Peace on duty at the time. The children were eventually taken to the Justice of the Peace on duty, who in turn sent some of them to the Rafael Ayau and to the Pre-egreso juvenile detention centres.

There is no information as to whether the children have been charged with any recognizable criminal offence. The testimony of the Covenant House staff member was reportedly not admitted by the Justice of the Peace because, it was reported, there was a "conflict of interests".

3. Felipe González Barrios ("Chiripa", aged 14) José Corrado Mendoza ("Olindo", aged 18)

Amnesty International is concerned at the alleged refusal of the National Police to investigate an incident in which two street children, Felipe González Barrios and José Corrado Mendoza, were severely beaten by two unidentified men, until a judge issued an order for them to do so. Amnesty International is concerned by reports that the initial refusal by the National Police to investigate the incident, enabled unidentified persons to subsequently remove the blood stains from the scene of the crime, where the children were found unconscious, thereby destroying potential incriminating evidence.

The incident occurred at about 10 pm on Monday 20 January. Felipe González and José Corrado Mendoza were walking together with Ludwin Gutiérrez, aged 16, along 11th Avenue between 12th and 13th street in zone 1 of Guatemala City, when two unidentified men wearing civilian clothes ran out of a house. The men reportedly stopped the street children without an apparent reason and threatened them at gunpoint. According to information received by Amnesty International, Ludwin Gutiérrez managed to escape while the unidentified men started to hit Felipe González and José Corrado Mendoza on the head and on other parts of their bodies with their guns. After the two men left, the two children were reportedly left bleeding on the pavement, and were helped by a passer-by who alerted the Fire Brigade. The children were taken unconscious to the San Juan de Dios General Hospital, where they stayed overnight. Felipe González was said to be unable to open his eyes and had to be led by hand, due to the fact that his face was very swollen. On 23 January 1992 Covenant House made a formal complaint to the National Police. The case is currently under the jurisdiction of the Juzgado 8o. de Paz Penal (8th Justice of the Peace in Criminal matters).

Felipe González has previously been the victim of several attacks. On 11 January 1992, he was beaten when, along with two other street children, Carlos Enrique Coy Po and Ludwin Gutiérrez, he was stopped by five individuals in plain clothes who accused the children of stealing. The assailants beat the three street children badly and then freed them. The next day, on 12 January 1992 Felipe González was again badly beaten by two men, whom he reported seeing emerging from a house in

Zone 1 of Guatemala City. He subsequently required hospital treatment from the beating he received.

Also, Felipe González was among three street children beaten on 7 November 1990 by thirteen members of SIPROCI, (four belonging to the National Police, five to the Treasury Police and four to the Mobile Military Police). The beating took place in front of a refuge run by Covenant House. A street educator, Axel Mejía, witnessed a member of the Treasury Police beating the children and intervened. The policeman then attempted to beat and then threatened Axel Mejía as he led the children back to Covenant House. Legal proceedings were subsequently initiated against one of the Treasury Police agents, identified as the principal aggressor, and against a member of the National Police. Axel Mejía gave evidence in the criminal proceedings against the accused agents. As a result of giving evidence, he and his family have been subjected to intimidation and death threats (see p. 12,13).

4. Elder Marroquín, 17

On 16 Elder Aníbal Marroquín was December 1991 Colindres returning to his Covenant House group home in Zone 6 of Guatemala City, when two uniformed policemen called out to him from behind. One of the policemen hit him over the head with his night stick. The boy lost consciousness and his shoes and wallet were stolen by the policemen. Following a medical examination, it was determined that the boy had a fractured nose from the blow he received. A formal complaint about the incident was made to the Procurador de los Derechos Humanos (Human Rights Procurator).

5. José Efraín Vásquez Solís, 16

José Efraín Vásquez Solís reported that he was walking in Zone 1 of Guatemala City, on 13 November 1991, at approximately 6.00 pm, when two vehicles pulled up in front of a restaurant and four armed men in civilian clothes jumped out. They fired some shots into the air. José Vásquez, who saw this from across the street, ran away and the men shouted at him to stop. The men caught up with José Vásquez, handcuffed him and forcibly shoved him into one of the vehicles, a white Volkswagen with four doors, and drove away. Inside the vehicle the men accused him of stealing money and beat him on the right side of his face with the butt of a pistol, as a result of which he lost consciousness. He reported that when he regained consciousness he believed he was in the area known as "Bosques de San Nicolás" in Zone 4 in the Mixco area of Guatemala City.[2] He was again beaten and as a result of the beating his left leg was fractured. José Vásquez also reported that the men burned him on his hands and fingers with a cigarette. The men then left and José Vásquez managed to reach other street youths, who assisted him to reach the Covenant House refuge. He was subsequently hospitalized, but left the hospital late that night with the help of a hospital worker after several private policemen came to the hospital asking for him.

---

[2] In June 1990, the tortured bodies of four street children were found in the Bosques de San Nicolás area. Two policemen are currently in prison, pending an appeal, after they were acquitted for their part in the murder of the children.

6. Walter Federico Flores, aged 17

At approximately 10:00 pm on 23 October 1991, two young men wearing uniforms similar to those worn by the cadets at the Escuela de Capacitación de la Policía (Police Cadets Training School), reportedly stopped Walter Federico Flores in the area known as Botellón, at 4th Avenue and 19th Street in Zone 1 of Guatemala City. They asked for Walter Flores' identification, but he did not want to show them his birth certificate because he was reportedly afraid the police might tear it up. Amnesty International has received reports that members of the police have torn up identification papers so that they can claim the children are over the age of 18. The two men subsequently hit Walter Flores on the head with their truncheons, and when he fell, they kicked him in different parts of his body, especially in the stomach and ribs. Walter Flores was also severely beaten on both arms and his left leg. He was left unconscious under a bridge in the same area, and regained consciousness at approximately 11:30 pm. Walter Flores, bleeding profusely from his head and right cheek, made his way to the Hogar Rafael Ayau, the government centre for abandoned children, where he was reportedly denied treatment. The boy went next to Covenant House where he was treated by a doctor. A formal complaint was made by Covenant House to the Magistratura Coordinadora de la Jurisdicción de Menores (Coordinating Magistrate in charge of Minors). The investigating judge ordered that a medical report be submitted. However, Covenant House reported that the case was not passed on to the corresponding court for further investigation.

II Street educators

In addition to the attacks on street children, Amnesty International has been very concerned at human rights violations, including abduction, torture, rape, intimidation and threats directed against staff, former staff of Covenant House, and their families. Many street educators would appear to be targeted because of their work with Covenant House and/or because they have acted as witnesses in some of the legal proceedings being initiated against members of the security forces.

1. Olga Odilia Jiménez Fajardo Adrián Medina

Three former staff workers with Covenant House, Olga Odilia Jiménez Fajardo, her common-law-husband Adrián Medina and a friend, Carolina García, left the country in January 1992, after a series of incidents, including death threats, abduction, continuous harassment and in one case rape dating from November 1990.

Olga Jiménez, a nurse who was temporarily working as a social worker with Covenant House, was at the San Juan de Dios Hospital when street child Nahamán Carmona lay wounded following the attack on him by policemen on 4 March 1990. Nahamán Carmona had spent over 32 hours under observation without having been seen by a doctor when he caught the attention of Olga Jiménez, whom he recognized. Olga Jiménez notified a doctor to examine Nahamán Carmona after he told her what had happened to him. (see Guatemala: Extrajudicial Executions and Human Rights Violations against Street Children, AI Index: AMR 34/37/90, July 1990)

In the first half of November 1990, three men driving a black American-style car without licence plates intercepted

Olga Jiménez in Zone 1 of Guatemala City, as she was walking home. They told her that she had a lot to tell them and that she should not have foreigners living in her house (a lawyer from Harvard University and an Australian journalist reporting on the political situation in Guatemala had reportedly been renting rooms in Olga Jiménez' house). According to her testimony to Covenant House, in September or October 1990 several calls were made asking for the foreigners who were living there. The callers warned them not to "brainwash" indigenous peoples ("que no mentalicen a los Indios") and not try to change them or they would "regret it".

On 7 March 1991, as Olga Jiménez was walking home with one of her four children, two men driving a four-door red car warned her that she would be abducted and sexually abused. They also told her that she was not being taken this time because her small daughter was with her. Two months later, on 15 May, an abduction attempt was made against Olga Jiménez. As she was on her way to the National Police hospital, where she worked at the time as a nurse, an unidentified man in plain clothes tried to grab her. She managed to escape by hitting her assailant in the stomach. She was, however, abducted on 27 May, as she was travelling between the San Juan de Dios Hospital and the National Police Hospital in Guatemala City. According to her testimony, four unidentified men got out of a four-door, American-style car, and forced her into the car. They said they wanted to talk to her. After about half an hour, she was made to get out of the car at the entrance of a place called Palencia in Guatemala City. They undressed her and told her to tell them what she knew. The asked her about several people who were living in her house and when she said she didn't know, one of the men went to hit her, but another told him to wait as in any case they were going to rape her. They again asked her about the people living in her house, about Covenant House and asked who she had spoken to in the hospital about Nahamán Carmona. One of the assailants then raped Olga Jiménez, while another went through her purse. When he saw her identification badge as a worker with the National Police Hospital they left the area. Olga Jiménez was subsequently operated on for the injuries she sustained to her vagina, as a result of the rape.

Olga Jiménez reported that a further attempt to abduct her was made on 29 August 1991. As she was walking towards the San Juan de Dios hospital two men in a blue car with polarized windows called her and asked her what time she would finish work. She replied that she had no time to stop, and made her way into the hospital, but one of the men grabbed her, and she hurt her arm against the car door in the struggle to escape.

Adrián Medina and Carolina García have also been reportedly harassed and threatened. These incidents would appear to be linked to their association with Covenant House. Carolina García was writing a university thesis on the subject of street children in Guatemala. Since November 1990, they and Olga Jiménez received repeated death threats by unknown individuals while they were on the street, as well as telephone calls to their homes. They were also repeatedly stopped on the street by unknown men, sometimes driving a black car. On one occasion a black vehicle containing two armed men reportedly stopped Adrián Medina as he was nearing the apartment he shared with Olga Jiménez. The men said they wanted to talk to him, and followed him for about three blocks until he arrived home. In January 1991 three men driving a black car assaulted the father of Adrián Medina near his home. The men approached and asked him if his name were Medina. When he said yes, the three men beat him. When Adrián Medina and his brother, who were at their father's home at the time, went out of the house, they saw a black car driving away.

Also in January 1991, Carolina García was approached by a man who told her to "shut up", as she was being watched "since the day she arrived to look after Nahamán" (Carmona). In March 1991, after Carolina García had moved in with Olga Jiménez and Adrián Medina, an unknown man called at the apartment and asked for "Adrián". When Olga Jiménez asked him who he wanted to see, he replied by saying that she was Olga. When she denied she was Olga, the person said "aunque traten de protegerse, aunque se unan, se los va a llevar la gran P... y los vamos a desaparecer o matar si no colaboran..." ("even though you try and protect yourselves, even though you stay together, something is going to happen to you...and we will kill you or "disappear" you if you do not cooperate").

2. Julio César López Héctor López

In separate but seemingly related incidents, three staff members of Covenant House were held up, beaten and robbed by armed men in civilian clothes in November 1991. Julio César López is a street educator, Héctor López works as a coordinator of street educators and Héctor Augusto Dionicio Godínez is a law student working with the Oficina de Apoyo Legal (Legal Aid Office) of Covenant House. From the testimonies of the three victims and the way in which the attacks were carried out, Covenant House has concluded that the incidents may have been linked. In the case of Héctor López, the assailants stated that they knew where he worked and lived, and made death threats against him. Héctor Dionicio was attacked in Guatemala City on 28 November 1991. He was reportedly grabbed by the neck from behind by an unidentified man. While he struggled to free himself, another man hit him on the left side of his head with a blunt instrument, which left him unconscious. Witnesses reported that while the attackers went through the wallet of the victim, one was reportedly heard to say "no nos equivocamos, éste hijo de la gran p... pertenece también a esa m..., tal vez así dejan de estarnos chingando." ("we were right, this son of a b.... also belongs to that s..t, perhaps now they will stop f... ing us around."). Covenant House has interpreted this as an indication that the attackers knew who they were targeting and that the motive for the attack was to intimidate Covenant House workers. According to the Héctor Dionicio the witnesses who helped him after the attack refused to give their names or addresses for fear of reprisals.

3. Axel Mejía

Axel Mejía Paiz is the supervisor of the Crisis Centre of the Covenant House refuge in Guatemala City. He was the principal witness to an incident which occurred on 7 November 1990, when thirteen members of the police unit SIPROCI, (four belonging to the National Police, five to the Treasury Police and four to the Mobile Military Police), beat three street children in front of a refuge run by Covenant House. Legal proceedings were subsequently initiated against one of the Treasury Police, identified as the principal aggressor, and Axel Mejía gave evidence in the criminal proceedings against the accused agent. Since that time, he has been constantly threatened and harassed, and in May 1991 he was forced to leave the country because of the level of harassment against him, but decided to return to Guatemala after several months, in order to continue his work with street children.

According to testimony given to Covenant House, on 12 March 1992, David Estuardo Mejía Paiz, Axel Mejía's brother, was abducted in Guatemala City.

He was walking towards his home in Zone 21, when a man in plain clothes put a gun to his head and told him not to resist or he would be shot. Three other men forced David Mejía into a black vehicle with polarized windows. He was then taken to a dark room and was held there for approximately forty-five minutes before being taken by one of the assailants to what David Mejía described as a passageway. He was told to telephone his brother Axel Mejía, but when he said his brother did not have a telephone, the assailant told him to telephone anyone who could pass on a message to his brother that "ni él ni su hermana tenían la culpa de lo que había hecho Axel" ("neither he nor his sister were to blame for what Axel had done"). David Mejía was then taken back to the dark room and blindfolded. One of the assailants threatened him and burned the right sleeve of David Mejía's sweater with a match, and all the while asked David Mejía if Axel Mejía was in Guatemala or if he had left the country. David Mejía then heard one of the assailants say to another "¿lo matamos, vos?" ("shall we kill him, then?"). David Mejía was released early on the morning of 13 March. Before his release the men told him that they were not going to kill him, but wanted it to be a warning to his brother of what they were capable of doing. During March 1992 the family was the subject of other incidents of serious harassment and their home was placed under surveillance.

III Witnesses to human rights violations

Amnesty International is concerned that in some cases, children who have given testimony of human rights violations by the security forces involving other street children have themselves been abused by the police, who apparently try to intimidate, and even eliminate those children who have incriminated them in crimes such as the beating, "disappearance", and extrajudicial execution of street children.

1. Vilma Jeannette Arévalo Deras and Ingri Luz Arévalo y Arévalo

The principal witness to the killing in March 1990 of street child Nahamán Carmona López, policewoman Vilma Jeannette Arévalo Deras, and her family have been consistently targeted throughout the criminal proceedings against the four policemen charged and recently convicted of homicide for the killing of Nahamán Carmona.

On 15 March 1992, Ingri Luz Arévalo y Arévalo, aged 18, a half-sister of Vilma Arévalo Deras, was attacked and raped by three unidentified men in the city of Jutiapa, department of Jutiapa. According to Ingri Arévalo, she was on her way to a local pharmacy at approximately 6.30 pm when three men grabbed her violently, covered her mouth and began slashing her arms and legs with a blade. The men then forced her into a car. They insulted her and drove off to an unknown location, where she was raped. One of the men said "vas a pagar los platos rotos de tu hermana y la próxima vez te vamos a matar" ("you are going to have to take the can for your sister"). Because it was dark when she was grabbed, Ingri Arévalo was unable to identify her attackers or the car they were driving. She was released, after being held for over an hour. Following her release, she was admitted for treatment to a private clinic in Guatemala City. The medical certificate issued by the clinic stated that the patient had bruises on different parts of her body, had wounds from a sharp instrument and that she had been violated. In mid-April 1992, Ingri Arévalo left the country. The attack and rape of Ingri Arévalo coincided with the re-trial taking place against the four policemen accused of the killing of Nahamán Carmona López. The sentences against the policemen in the first trial were overturned in July 1991 on technical grounds and a re-trial ordered. (See Section: Update on Criminal Proceedings against those responsible for human rights violations against street children)

Vilma Arévalo Deras reported being subjected to threats and intimidation after she testified against four policemen charged with the killing of Nahamán Carmona in the original trial and in March 1991 left Guatemala with two of her children to seek political asylum in another country.

2. Francisco Tziac

Seventeen-year-old street child Francisco Tziac, of the Cakchiquel ethnic group, is a key witness in the legal proceedings against four policemen currently serving prison sentences of between 12 and 18 years for the killing of his friend, Nahamán Carmona López.[3] Nahamán Carmona died on 14 March 1990, and since his killing Francisco Tziac has been singled out by uniformed and plainclothes police, and has been abducted, beaten and threatened.

On 10 April 1990 several children who had witnessed the attack on Nahamán made a declaration to an examining magistrate. In their statement, the children gave a detailed description of the assailants. Approximately month after giving the declaration Francisco Tziac was attacked and beaten by two policemen in Guatemala City. Several days later, he

---

[3] Four policemen were originally sentenced in March 1991 to between 10 and 15 years for the killing of street child Nahamán Carmona in March 1990. In July 1991 the sentences were overturned and a re-trial was ordered. In April 1992 the four policemen were sentenced to between 12 and 18 years. (See Section: Update on criminal proceedings against those responsible for human rights violations)

was again singled out for attack by a policeman who pulled him around by his hair.

On 14 July 1990 two uniformed policemen wearing the type of boots reportedly used only by motorcycle policemen stopped Francisco Tziac in the city centre, and asked his name. Before leaving they told him "no sólo nosotros tenemos tu nombre, sino que one muchos policías, no queremos verte más por ese sector y por ninguna parte de la zona uno, y si te vemos te vamos a matar" ("not just us, but many policemen have your name, and we don't want to see you around here or any place in Zone 1, and if we see you, we'll kill you.")

On 29 May 1991 Francisco Tziac was abducted for a period of several hours by two unknown men, who grabbed him between 13th and 14th street, in Zone 1 of Guatemala City. He was bundled into a blue car and taken to a place unknown to him, where he was severely beaten, before being released in Zone 19 of the city.

On 18 December 1991, Francisco Tziac was again abducted by two men as he was walking in Zone 1 of Guatemala City with two other street children. He was forced into a pick-up and taken to the Puente Olímpico (Olímpico Bridge). There, he later reported, he was thrown out of the pick-up, kicked and insulted by one of the men, who he stated had an identification tag around his neck similar to those used by the armed forces. This same man then took a gun out of his holster and said "Aquí te vas a morir..." ("here you are going to die..."), but the second man intervened and said that Francisco Tziac should not be killed. While the two men argued Francisco Tziac took the opportunity to escape and fled to Covenant House.

Amnesty International believes this latest attack on Francisco Tziac was designed to intimidate witnesses called to give further evidence at the re-trial of four policemen for the killing of Nahamán Carmona.

On the afternoon of 7 April 1992 Francisco Tziac arrived at the Legal Aid office of Covenant House. He was bleeding from his nose and mouth. He said that he had just been attacked by three armed men who caught him stealing from a car. The child said that the men took him to a house on 5th Avenue, Zone 1 of Guatemala City, handcuffed him and beat him on the back, chest, arms and face. According to his testimony, his assailants asked him about Bruce Harris, and said that it was Bruce Harris who made the street children steal. The men then released him, and Francisco Tziac made his way to the Legal Aid office, where Covenant House staff took him to hospital. According to Covenant House staff, when waiting at the emergency ward, a National Police agent came to interrogate Francisco Tziac about what had happened to him. When the child told her that he was caught stealing, the agent told him that had happened because street children were always stealing. Francisco Tziac, left the hospital very upset, but was persuaded to return by one of the Covenant House staff who accompanied him. The other worker asked the police agent to change the tone of her interrogation, as she was upsetting the child, but she reportedly continued the same line of questioning, and told Francisco Tziac that he would have to wait at least two hours before being attended to. The child left the hospital again, and went into hiding.

3. Axel Mejía

Alex Rolman Castillo Morales, a 19-year-old street youth, is a key witness in a case being brought by the Ministerio Público (Public Ministry), against a private security agent currently imprisoned, serving a 10-year sentence for the murder of 15-year-old street child Francisco Chacón Torres. Francisco Chacón died after being shot while walking in Zone 9 of Guatemala City on 28 April 1991.[4] Alex Castillo Morales who was with Francisco Chacón at the time he was killed, has given evidence to the Juzgado Tercero de Primera Instancia Penal de Instrucción (Third Criminal Examining Court of the First Instance), who are hearing the case. On 19 November 1991, at approximately 2.00pm at the corner of 18th Street and 10th Avenue in Zone 1 of Guatemala City, Alex Castillo Morales was walking towards the centre of the city, when a white covered van with polarized windows, pulled up beside him and a man in plain clothes asked him his name. Alex Castillo was forcefully shoved into the back of the van. The victim later reported that there were four men in the van, all in plain clothes. Two men in the rear of the van began beating Alex Castillo on his back with a wooden club and they took him to the area near the Mateo Flores gymnasium in Zone 5 of the city. After they had beaten him, they told him not to tell anyone about the incident and not to try and get them into trouble. They then threw him out of the back doors of the van, and held on to him for several meters while the van was moving, dragging him along the ground, causing scrapes to his back and arm.

Update on Criminal Proceedings against those responsible for human rights violations against street children.

There are currently 6 arrest warrants as well as more than 65 pending law suits against more than 50 National Police and four members of the PMA, pending with the Guatemalan courts. Amnesty International is concerned that in many cases investigations carried out by the authorities are incomplete or contain irregularities. In many cases there were long delays by

---

[4] See Guatemala: Apparent Extrajudicial Execution of Francisco Chacón Torres, AI Index: AMR 34/24/91 of June 1991

the National Police in executing arrest warrants issued against members of the security forces. Amnesty International is further concerned that the failure by the authorities to identify the perpetrators and bring them to justice could make it appear that the official legal and security apparatus condones such acts, and could thus serve to encourage further such abuses. Only in isolated cases have investigations resulted in the prosecution of those responsible, and in several other cases irregularities in judicial proceedings have been alleged.

Amnesty International is urging the Guatemalan government to ensure that the pending cases against members of the security forces for a wide range of abuses of street children, are dealt with speedily and correctly by the courts.

Members of the security forces arrested in connection with cases of human rights violations against street children

1. Killing of Nahamán Carmona López

Thirteen-year-old Nahamán Carmona López was attacked by four policemen two years ago on 4 March 1990, and died as a result of the beatings he received.

In March 1991 four Guatemalan police officers who were accused of the killing of Nahamán Carmona López were brought to trial and sentenced to prison terms of between 10 and 15 years. However, on 19 July 1991, the sentences were overturned by the Third Chamber of the Appeals Court (Sala Tercera de la Corte de Apelaciones) on technical grounds.

A transcript of the sentence made available to Amnesty International indicated that the annulment of the sentences was due to "the violation of ... essential formalities in the proceedings" ("la violación de ... formalidades esenciales del proceso") which, in the Court's view, gave grounds for the annulment of the sentences. The transcript stated that in the order initiating criminal procedures, the hour indicated for the killing of Nahamán was at 2.30 am, while it had been established that the killing took place a 0.20 am on 4 March 1990. A fine of 20 Quetzales (US$4.00) was imposed on the sentencing judge. According to the information made available to AI, the charges against the policemen still applied, and a retrial was ordered by the Appeals Court. The policemen remained in jail, pending the re-trial.

The new case was reopened before the Juzgado Quinto de Primera Instancia Penal de Sentencia (Fifth Criminal Sentencing Court of the 1st Instance), and new evidence admitted. On 28 April 1992, the four Guatemalan police officers were found guilty of homicide by the Fifth Criminal Sentencing Court of the 1st Instance, and sentenced to terms of between 12 and 18 years. Three of the four policemen were sentenced to 12 years and 6 months and the fourth to 18 years and 3 months. According to the information we have received, the sentence also bans the policemen from holding a public post. The policemen are currently appealing the sentence.

2. Apparent extrajudicial execution of Francisco Chacón Torres, 15

Amnesty International learned that in March 1992 the Juzgado Primero de Primera Instancia Penal de Sentencia (First Criminal Court of the First Instance) sentenced a private security agent to ten years' imprisonment, non-commutable, for the murder on 28 April 1991 of 15-year-old street child Francisco Chacón Torres. The mother of Francisco Chacón Torres was awarded 10,000 Quetzales (1US$ = 5 Quetzales approximately) by the court.

According to the court transcript made available to Amnesty International, the security agent worked for an unlicenced private security firm owned by an Israeli citizen who admitted in court he was a "collaborator" of G-2, Guatemala's military intelligence, and a military commissioner (a civilian auxiliary to the military).

3. Apparent extrajudicial execution of Anstraum Aman Villagrán Morales, 17 and the abduction of eight youths in June 1990

On 17 January 1992 two members of the National Police and a civilian, indicted in April 1991 in connection with the killing by uniformed policemen of 17-year-old Anstraum Aman Villagrán Morales on 25 June 1990, were acquitted by the Juzgado Tercero de Sentencia (Third Criminal Court) "por falta de plena prueba para condenarlos" ("for lack of evidence to convict them"). The policemen and the civilian were acquitted despite that fact that a ballistics' report had apparently established that the bullet used to kill Anstraum Villagrán Morales had been fired from a gun issued to one of the policemen charged with his murder. There are allegations that this evidence was suppressed in court. The three defendants were also indicted for the abduction of eight youths in two separate incidents in June 1990. Several of these youths were found dead after their abduction, their bodies showing signs of brutal torture. Amnesty International is concerned that irregularities in the investigation may have led to the acquittal of the three defendants. The Public Ministry is appealing against the acquittal.

4. Apparent extrajudicial execution of Marvin Oswaldo de la Cruz Melgar, 13

On 8 July 1991, a three-year suspended sentence was imposed on two former policemen, detained in connection with the killing of street child Marvin de la Cruz Melgar was upheld on appeal. Both former policemen were found guilty of culpable homicide and cover-up by the Fifth Sentencing Court for Penal matters. One of the policemen was ordered to pay the equivalent of US$400 in civil damages and the other US$10 court costs. They were both released, pending appeal.

5. Beating of Walter Chapetón, 13 and Víctor Manuel Castellanos, 14

On 23 March 1992 two members of the PMA charged with abuse of authority for the beating on 1 January 1991 of Walter Chapetón and Víctor Manuel Castellanos were released by the Fiscalía Militar (Military Prosecutor's office). Despite evidence submitted by a counsellor from Covenant House who witnessed the abuse and statements by other members of the PMA, one of them was acquitted, and the other one was released conditionally on bail with security, pending appeal.

6. Beating of William Jonathan Ortiz López, 14

On 22 February 1992 a member of the National Police was found guilty and was sentenced to 25 days' imprisonment, commutable, for the beating of 14-year-old street child Jonathan Ortiz López on 5 July 1990. The defendant was also fined 200 Quetzales. There was no appeal against the sentence. The policeman had been taken into custody charged with abuse against individuals on 22 December 1991, but only after a number of arrest warrants had been issued, and a series of complaints regarding the delays in carrying out the arrest orders had been lodged by Covenant House. William Jonathan Ortiz López had reportedly been grabbed by two members of the National Police from the 7th Precinct in Guatemala City and forced to the ground. One of the policemen grabbed a wire cable and started whipping Jonathan Ortiz on the back and shouting "You are a friend of Nahamán, and we are friends of the policemen in jail." The policemen then forced Jonathan Ortiz to drink sewage from an open drain by the side of the road."

III. Ak' Tenamit Association

Ak' Tenamit is a Guatemalan NGO working since its origin in the 1990s on sustainable development and integrating more than thirty Maya-Q'eqchi' communities of Río Dulce National Park area, benefiting more than 8,000 people. Its areas of work are health, education, community development, sustainable agriculture, handicrafts and ecotourism, all of which are based on the principles of gender equity, respect for nature and the Mayan worldview. The restaurant operates as a school for young Mayan-Q'eqchi who study sustainable tourism, income-support education activities, and community development association. Ak' Tenamit is one of the few destinations that is certified as a sustainable destination in recognition of the minimal impact caused by its activities to the environment and local culture.

Barbara H Mullen Reed, EdD

IV. H.O.M.E. (Homeworkers Organized for More Employment)

H.O.M.E. is a cooperative community dedicated to economic and social reconstruction. It began in 1970 in rural Maine as an outlet for homeworkers' crafts. H.O.M.E. has expanded to include a free health clinic; soup kitchen; food bank; homeless shelters; a learning center with daycare, literacy, and GED tutoring; house construction; alternative high school and college-level programs; job and craft training; pottery, leather, wood, and weaving shops; recovery barn; greenhouses and farmers' market; sawmill and shingle mill.

V. Status of International Adoptions

Note: On January 1, 2008 the government of Guatemala officially closed international adoptions. See attached https://www.brandeis.edu/investigate/adoption/guatemala.html

www.ingramcontent.com/pod-product-compliance
Lightning Source LLC
Chambersburg PA
CBHW070104080526
44586CB00013B/1177